Unwrapping Little Gifts

Making the Gospel Come Alive for Children

Mary Budden
Nancy Baize

Resource Publications, Inc.
San Jose, California

Editorial director: Kenneth Guentert
Contributing editors: Linda Murphy for the
    Benedictine Resource Center; Susan Pellant
    for Resource Publications, Inc.
Managing editor: Elizabeth J. Asborno
Editorial assistant: Mary Ezzell
Artist: George Collopy

Reprint Department
Resource Publications, Inc.
160 E. Virginia Street #290
San Jose, CA 95112-5876

**Library of Congress
Cataloging in Publication Data**
Budden, Mary.
    Unwrapping little gifts : making the Gospel
come alive for children / Mary Budden,
Nancy Baize.
        p.   cm.
    Includes bibliographical references and
index.
    ISBN 0-89390-290-X
    1. Puppet theater in public worship—
Catholic Church. 2. Puppet plays,
American. 3. Bible plays, American.
4. Children's mass. 5. Catholic Church—
Liturgy. I. Baize, Nancy. II. Title.
BX2238.4.B83   1994
246'.7—dc20   94-32839

Printed in the United States of America

98 97 96 95 94 | 5 4 3 2 1

Hope is the thing with feathers
That perches in the soul,
And sings the tune without words
And never stops at all.

Emily Dickinson

To Mom and Dad,
who helped us unwrap
our little gifts

From the Mouths of Babes:

After hearing the congregation say,
"Only say the word and I shall be healed,"
our little one asked: "Mom, what's the word?"

A youngster was asked,
"What are the most important words said during the consecration?"
Her eager response: "There's enough for everybody?"

If it's supposed to be Good News,
why does our minister always yell and scream?

This book was written to try to bring logical answers
to these and countless other questions posed
by children trying desperately to "belong"
to organized faith communities.

To these littlest ones—
whose unbounded joy and innocent faith
are the characteristics most surely
commended to us when Jesus said,
"Unless you become as these little ones,
you cannot enter the kingdom of heaven"—
the pages of this manual are dedicated.

Contents

Acknowledgments

Our special thanks to all who have shared their little gifts with us in creating this manual, but especially to:

- Carmen Ortiz
- Lupe Ruiz
- Dorothy Ybarra
- Sr. Dot O'Meara, CSB
- David Alonzo
- Imelda Morales
- The Good News family of puppeteers
- The countless little people who shared thoughts and talents
- The St. Brigid Catholic Church Community of San Antonio, Texas
- Benedictine Resource Center
- And, most of all, our own children, our domestic church, who helped us recapture our little.

Preface: A Little Parable

Once upon a time, there was a kingdom, right here on earth. In this kingdom, there lived many people, both big and little. Once a week, all the people of the kingdom were invited to come to a celebration. All the people (well, almost all) would gather together for the celebration. You see, at the celebration there were many gifts to be unwrapped and some of the big people would unwrap a few of their gifts. The little people, always filled with anticipation, would come to the celebration, hoping to unwrap one of their gifts too and be able to go home as excited as the big people.

However, once all the people got to the celebration, the turmoil would start. A group of big people would welcome everyone as they arrived. The celebration would begin with a procession down through the middle of the people, who would be standing and singing a joyful song. Mostly big people were part of this procession. Some carried candles and others were selected to read the stories. They all walked together with the leader to the front of the gathering place. The little people reached for their songbooks but found the words were just too big for them. So, they directed their attention to the procession only to discover that they were too little to see over the big people. When all the people sat down, the little people knew right away that it was story time. The gathering place became very quiet and one of the big people stood to read. It didn't take very long for the little people to realize that the words of the story were just too big. Then everyone would stand and the leader would read a special story. Usually the story was told so that the big people were the only ones to understand it. But, at this particular celebration, the leader read a story about little people that said: "Unless you become like little people, you cannot enter the kingdom." This was very confusing for the little people and it made them wonder if the big people the leader was taking about had lost some of their "little." After the storytelling, the leader would talk to the people about the stories.

At this time, the little people would grow very restless, mostly because these stories were told in words too big for them to enjoy. Usually this was also the time they would begin their own celebration games. Some of the little people would ask the big people for some gum or candy or a tissue. Others found fun things to do with songbooks. If there were any pieces of paper around, some would create airplanes or find a pencil to draw some magnificent work of art (at least it was magnificent in their little eyes). Then a few would jump up and run out for a cold drink of water or something else. Occasionally, there were "war" games like pinching, pulling hair or punching. "War" games almost always produced a lot of crying and screaming. Then the big people began their usual "shshshing" and some of the big people would actually yank the little people out of their chairs and take them out of the gathering place into the outer hall. Some of the big people smiled because they knew what would happen next! Echoes of spankings and loud crying could be heard.

Shortly after that, the big people gift-bearers carried up the bread and wine for the meal, along with the baskets of money they had collected from all the people, big and little. The leader then said a prayer of thanksgiving over the gifts. The bread and wine were blessed and the bread broken in preparation for it being shared by almost everyone, even some of the older little people. A special prayer that asked for peace to come to all the inhabitants of the kingdom was said by everyone. The little people especially enjoyed this because they were allowed to join in too. After this prayer, everyone would turn to each other and shake hands or give hugs. During this special time, the little people noticed that everyone was smiling and happy, even the big people who hardly ever smiled during these celebrations. Suddenly there was silence and the leader invited all the people to come up and share in this meal. The little-little people had to stay in their seats while all the big people, along with the older-little people, went to share in the meal.

After the meal, the leader would bless the people and send them out into the kingdom.

After the celebration, all the big people gathered outside and discussed the stories they had just heard, as well as some of their own stories. The little people were full of energy and enjoyed running and jumping around, and besides, they didn't understand the stories anyway. Hardly anybody had ever taken the time to explain why they had come to the celebration. Maybe someday they would have more big in them, but for now they were just little people.

The End

Why Us? Why This *Little Book?*

When our sons crafted super jet airplanes out of the Sunday bulletin—and flew them during liturgy...

When we held our breath in anxious fear at their possible flight plans...

When they told us it was not polite to eat in front of others, and *they* wanted to share in the Eucharist, too...

When they wanted to know, "What's the word?" "What's the word?" each time we proclaimed, "...but only say the *word* and I shall be healed..."

When we began to see through the eyes of these little people what worship and liturgy looked like to them...

We discovered why they were making so many trips to the drinking fountain (it wasn't water they thirsted for; it was a thirst to participate, to partake, to understand).

We became involved in creating a worship experience that met their needs, not ours.

We experienced young people unwrapping their own gifts for liturgy and worship, claiming ownership in the rituals of their faith.

We saw the face of God—
    alive and innocent,
        giving freely of time and talent,
            unprejudiced and joy-filled...
                ...and of such is the kingdom!

A Little Background: How We Began Our Puppet Ministry

Several years ago, we were asked by the Director of Religious Education at our parish to create a puppet ministry. We asked a few children who were interested to help us work the puppets. And so, we began—with practically no knowledge nor experience in using this medium. We felt that if we were to do a good job we had to learn all we could about this ministry. We found that many other denominations had used puppets for many years in working with children. Puppets would aid teachers in helping children learn bible verses and act out stories from the bible. Most of the resources we found focused on this aspect of puppetry, but we felt our gift was to focus on the values, the common life experiences, the moral of the story for every day. With a small allowance from our director, we purchased four puppets—a mother, father, boy and girl—from Pakaluk Puppets of Fredericksburg, Texas. Owners Rose and Fred Knapp design and create each puppet and stock their shop from floor to ceiling with their creations. In addition to pre-made puppets, they offer custom-made designs as well. For more information, please turn to the Resources section.

We named our four puppets the *Good News Family* and officially began this ministry by placing an announcement in the church bulletin stating that a new family was coming to our parish and would be present at the next 9:30 Sunday liturgy. We used *"Love Makes People Happy"* as our theme, and for a symbol we decided on inflatable pink hearts. For two weeks prior to the liturgy, we decorated bulletin boards in the parish hall, church building and classrooms with the hearts and a note indicating that a new family was joining our faith community. That Sunday, we used the hearts to decorate the worship space. The script was simple, touching on the need to let others know we

love them, not just on special days, but every day. As background music played, the "puppets" asked everyone to turn to the person on either side and give each a hug. We concluded with the song *"Love Makes People Happy."* Adults and children enjoyed it, and so it began.

Our puppeteers ranged in age from ten to twelve. Their first year's work consisted of shows during religious education classes and at children's liturgies throughout the year. The audiences in the religion classes ranged from preschoolers to third graders. Afterward, we discovered that the attention span for the preschoolers required us to shorten the scripts and use songs with a lot of repetition. We also discovered that taping the script ahead of time allowed the puppeteers to concentrate completely on the puppet's movements and character, which greatly improved the quality of the shows.

When the first season came to an end, it was evident that we needed many more puppeteers to continue this ministry. We invited fourth, fifth and sixth graders and their parents to a two-hour workshop. We asked the children to share why they wanted to be a part of the puppet ministry and we gave them some hands-on experience with the puppets. The veteran puppeteers showed them some of the techniques they had learned. The children practiced a script and then recorded it to see how their voices sounded. We asked the children to consider what puppet ministry involved and discuss it with their parents. If both they and their parents agreed to all the aspects of puppet ministry, both had to sign the commitment paper we gave them and return it by a set date.

We organized the volunteers into groups of four—usually two boys and two girls. Each fall we planned the puppet shows for the upcoming religious education year. After scheduling the performances and coordinating the themes for classes and children's liturgies, we assigned teams for each performance. Using this team approach helped to prevent burnout among the volunteers. On occasion, we even took our show "on the road" to other parishes, nursing homes and hospitals.

To prepare for a particular puppet performance, we mailed copies of the script to each of the team members and included two dates for rehearsals. This gave team members the opportunity to practice ahead of time at home, using a plain old sock as the puppet. At the first practice, the team concentrated all their energies on the script. The team approach enabled those who were more expressive to assist those who were timid. Those who were timid taught the extroverts a little gentleness and patience. We rehearsed the lines until everyone felt comfortable with them. After taking a short break, we recorded the show and listened together to the finished product. If all were pleased with the results, the practice was over.

A few days before the performance, we met again to practice with the puppets. Each time we reminded the puppeteers that, once they put their hands inside the puppet, they stopped being themselves and took on the personality of the puppet. This was especially helpful for the quieter, more timid puppeteers, allowing them to "get lost" in their new character. Even basic activities, such as waving hello or hugging, took practice. Since each performance usually ended with a song or taped music, the characters also had to learn to sing and sway to the music. A final practice took place about thirty minutes before the performance. After going through the routine one final time, we all held hands and prayed that our work would allow the Good News to touch the hearts of all those present.

The first stage we used was an old puppet stage, constructed of three sheets of particle board joined together with hinges. The middle piece was cut out in a scalloped design, and the two side pieces served as supports for the middle. We set the stage atop a long table covered with a plain white tablecloth. The children who had volunteered to help us sat on a bench behind the table to remain out of sight. After working with various designs for the puppet stages, we found the one we liked the best was a larger stage made from white plastic PVC pipes, which can be purchased at lumber or hardware stores. We recommend the 1½- or 2-inch pipe. Pipe elbows are used for the corners. Other items needed to complete the project include: PVC cement, a hacksaw and tape measure. We found this particular style to be very portable and easy to set up. The curtains, which we made from heavy, wrinkle-free polyester double knit, slide easily over the pipe. It is important to make sure that the material is not see-through. The stage we created cost approximately $100.

By numbering the pieces of PVC pipe, we were able to cut the set-up time significantly. Although the pipes fit snugly into the elbows, we always carried electrical or duct tape to secure parts that might become wobbly. Everyone on the puppet team helped in the process of setting up and taking down the stage.

Scriptwriting: Breaking Open the Good News

When we set out to write a script based on a particular gospel reading, we always began by reading the scripture passage several times. Reflectively, we opened our hearts to the Word. Then we gathered resources to assist us in this work. Settling on one or two words or ideas, we tried to weave it into a story. The core of the story would be centered around a child's experience—a situation with which a child could easily identify. We were also careful to write it in a language and style comfortable for the young. An example will illustrate the process and end result.

"The Lost Sheep"

This parable reinforces the image of Jesus as a loving and caring friend. In our script, we bring the story to the children's level by having the little girl puppet very upset about losing her favorite stuffed animal, Lovey Lamb. Her brother is very reluctant to help her, as she has a whole room full of stuffed animals. The family of puppets all go out into the rainy night to help her search for her favorite toy. They see how important this toy is to her. They are all very happy when it is found. Then, the dad shares the story of the lost sheep and how Jesus loves us so much and we are so special to him. To tie the story together and restate the message, we end the script with suggested music selections that could be sung by the children.

Another method we used is the Praxis method, designed by Thomas H. Groome in his book, *Christian Religious Education: Sharing our Story and Vision*. This method involves several steps in somewhat of a problem-solving process. The first step involves naming the present action or experience. The second is reflecting on what exactly has happened in the message or story. Third, a dialogue is established to identify a Christian tradition or scripture verse which helps us to understand the situation. Finally, a more careful understanding of the scripture passage in the light of our present experience occurs, allowing all to reach their own decisions and to grow along their journey.

The little boy and little girl puppets come running on stage very upset about a big fight in their neighborhood. They share their dilemma with their parents and, in turn, the parents share their own experience with fights they have had. Then the parents talk about being peacemakers for Jesus and changing their hearts. At this point, the boy and girl puppets make a choice about what they will do to stop the fighting and restore peace in the neighborhood. This method not only helps the children but also the parents. It allows the children the opportunity to decide how they can incorporate the Good News message into their own lives.

Dr. Megan McKenna, a gifted storyteller and lecturer, is the creator of still another tool used in the development of our scripts. Using a seven-step format, she assisted us in breaking open the Good News. This format is especially helpful in pulling out the essential word or verse to be used in the scriptwriting. The questions to be asked in studying scripture in this format are contained in the reproducible handout on the next page.

Sometimes we began our practices on the scripts with time for the puppeteers to give input about their lines, the story itself, or the message that we might have wanted to impart. Providing the puppeteers with an active role in the creation of the scripts allowed the young people to claim ownership of the process. Often, their ideas were incredibly insightful and more appropriately geared to the audience than our draft.

Once we had established a theme, drafted a script and selected appropriate music, we took that product to the people who would be involved at the parish level. This was a critical part of the process. Effective and clear lines of communication kept everyone involved and open to the activities of the children and puppeteers.

Scriptwriting Worksheet: Breaking Open the Good News

First, read the passage below not for information but for conversion, to call each other to challenge, change, repent, reconcile your lives and encourage each other to become true disciples. Then answer the questions.

Scripture passage: _____

1. What do you feel when you read the scripture?

2. Do you feel nervous or uncomfortable as you read anything in this scripture? Why might that be?

3. What are the who, what, where, when, how and why of the passage?

4. In light of the three previous questions, what are you going to do to change—to make this passage come true in your life? Be simple, practical and concrete.

5. We are prophets by baptism and confirmation. What does the scripture call you to do in the areas of peace, justice and care for the poor?

6. What is the church, as community, called to do in this passage?

7. What in the reading gives you hope?

Introduction

So, you're interested in helping children develop expressions of their faith? Of course you are. That's why you picked up this book and are looking at it right now. Unfortunately, there is no magic formula, no "operating manual" to tell you exactly how to accomplish this without fail. A variety of resources are available and each one has valuable ideas and materials that can be useful. As anyone experienced in parish ministry will tell you, each parish community is unique and what works well for one parish may not work well in another. However, the basic ideas and materials can be adapted to the particular needs and circumstances of each parish. Perhaps one of the most important things to keep in mind is to have a variety of approaches. Canon Law is very clear in pointing out *"that the faith of young people and adults* be fortified, enlightened and developed *through various means and endeavors"* (#777-5, emphasis added).

> Catechetical formation is to be given by *employing all those helps, teaching aids and communications media which appear to be more effective* in enabling the faithful in light of their characteristics, talents, age and conditions of life, to learn the Catholic teaching more fully and practice it more suitably" (#779, emphasis added).

It should be a source of encouragement to realize that while there is no magic formula there are wonderful resources available that you can use in your parish in whatever way they are most appropriate.

This book will provide you with materials that will help you to give the children in your parish opportunities to express their faith. While these materials have been developed from a Roman Catholic perspective, the scripts focus on basic Christian values common to all denominations. These scripts, which are gathered together by theme, seek to capture "The Little" we often leave behind as we grow into adult Christians. Using settings and situations with which children easily identify, the scripts enable both young and old to discover connections between their faith and their everyday lives. Most of the scripts list Scripture passages related to the theme, making it easier to coordinate the themes with the Sunday readings. There are even some scripts that are particularly suitable for parishes with Hispanic members. Each script has suggestions for songs that can be easily sung by children or played from cassettes. Simple handouts that the children can either do themselves or take home are provided for each script. Originally designed for use as puppet scripts, these scripts can be easily adapted for use as playlets or stories. The scripts can be used as supplements to Religious Education classes, as special presentations throughout the year, as part of a Liturgy of the Word for Children program or as part of a special Liturgy with Children.

Those who have had the privilege of working with children know what truly wonderful gifts they have to share. Their joy, openness, honesty, sense of awe, and enthusiastic delight in simple, everyday things can teach us so much. Little people need to know that they belong and that they have gifts to share. Allowing children to become active, visible participants in our faith communities not only enriches us but also assures them of their value and importance as members of the community. To paraphrase St. Paul, we are all members of the same body and each member, from the greatest to the least, is important and needed and each has been given gifts to share with the whole body. May these pages help you unwrap the gifts of the littlest ones in your community.

Puppet Ministry

If you are interested in starting a puppet ministry, these scripts will give you an excellent start. You will notice that no names have been given to the characters. This was done so that you would have the freedom to name your own puppets according to whatever cultural and ethnic backgrounds make up your parish community. Or, if you prefer, they can simply be Mom and Dad, Grandma, etc. You may also want to consider purchasing puppets that are culturally suitable for your community. Another important thing to note is that our Good News puppet family is not necessarily the model of your "average" family. If you have many single-parent families in your community, you may want to adjust the scripts accordingly. The last thing you want to do is make someone uncomfortable because he or she is different from the family portrayed. Variety helps to avoid stereotypes, even in puppet ministry.

However, if you are thinking that a puppet ministry is a bit ambitious for you right now, don't make the mistake of thinking that this resource is not for you. While most of the scripts contained in this book were written for puppet shows, each one has been adapted so it can be acted out in skit or drama form, or, with a little adjustment, presented as a story.

Story Time

Another easy adaptation is to use a script for a "story time" narrative. Begin by setting the scene and adding comments about the feeling and actions of the characters. For example, if you were going to use the script "Gift of Love" in this way, you might begin with:

Jimmy was staring intently out the living room window. Meanwhile his sister, Alice, kept trying to peek over his shoulder. "Oh, I can hardly wait a minute longer. Are they here yet?" Alice asked. "They should be here anytime now!" Jimmy said. Just then, they saw a car pull up in front of their house. An elderly man and woman got out and began to walk up to the house. "They're here! Oh, they're finally here!" Alice squealed happily as she ran to open the front door.

The narrative can be presented along with the use of a story board, which involves taking cutouts of people and important objects in the script and placing them on a felt board while telling the story. If you have someone with a talent for drawing, you can make pictures of the scenes in the script and display them on a newsprint pad or overhead projector. If you choose to use pictures, keep in mind the size of your audience and be sure the pictures are large enough to be seen by all. When using pictures from a book, contact the publisher to obtain permission to transfer them onto slides. A local photo-finishing store can transfer the pictures onto slides for a minimal cost.

Skits for Special Programs

Sometimes it can be helpful to bring together children of different ages or grade levels for a special session together. Some of the older children may enjoy doing the script as a little skit to present to the group. Others may be "in charge" of making the handouts, which can then be presented to everyone in a special ceremony at the end of the session. This could also be done as a special session for the parents and other interested adults. The children could be assigned specific tasks and roles according to abilities. Aside from the obvious things such as being characters in the playlet or making the "gifts" to be given at the end, there are numerous other ways to ensure that all the children have an active part. Some could be greeters, who welcome the parents as they arrived. Others might be ushers, who escort the parents to their seats. Those who like to sing could be the choir and lead the group in an appropriate song. Still others could be "presenters," who hand out the gifts at the end. Consider inviting *all* of the parishioners to attend, not just those with children. Having the children do a presentation for the adults of the parish will not only help the children feel more involved in the parish community but it can also provide a learning experience for the adults.

A Little Word about Handouts

Although optional, the handouts are a good way to enhance the message with something physical that the children can hold or color or cut out—in short, make their very own. Encourage the children to display their handouts at home, where everyone will be sure to see them during the week. As families go through their busy week, the handouts become an excellent way to remind everyone to live their faith daily.

Handout suggestions are given for each presentation. Sometimes more than one handout is suggested; as these are options for handouts, you may choose to do one or more. The instructions and patterns for the handouts are on a separate page following each presentation. Because some handout pages have text printed on the other side, you will want to photocopy these pages before cutting out the patterns.

Time constraints may make it impractical to have students actually "do" the suggested projects within the session time. In that case, the symbols can be done ahead of time and presented to the children at the end of the session. Or, perhaps an even better option, give the children the project to do at home and have them share what they did in the session with their families. It would probably be helpful to give the parents a brief handout explaining the theme and the project to be done at home. If the project is done at home, you may want to ask the children to share what they did or bring the project back to the next session to show the other children.

Keep in mind that, while helpful, handouts can be time-consuming. Be sure to plan ahead to avoid having to cut out three hundred red hearts the night before you need to use them! You may want to have some volunteers prepare the handouts for you. Instead of looking to the parents for help with this, consider having older children or teenagers do it as a special project. You might even want to look into asking some of the older parishioners, especially those who may be housebound, if they would be interested in helping to prepare the handouts.

If you are doing these as part of a Liturgy of the Word for Children, give some thought to having the children pick up their handouts after the Mass. Depending upon the type of handout, it may be a disastrous distraction to have the children bring them back into the main church. Sometimes, it may be appropriate to have the children bring the handouts in and place them in a special basket in front of the altar as part of the presentation of the gifts.

A Little Encouragement

We could never have written this book without lots of little encouragements from those around us. Hopefully you, too, will be blessed with encouraging words from those in your community, those who share in your vision of quality celebration with children.

The clipping which follows appeared in our local newspaper. Its author, columnist Blair Corning, encouraged us to share its message with you. It was sent to her by a young man named Phillip Brewer, who clearly knows just what is needed to accomplish any task.

Strong enough to be weak;
Successful enough to fail;
Busy enough to say, "I don't know";
Rich enough to be poor;
Right enough to say, "I'm wrong";
Compassionate enough to discipline;
Conservative enough to give freely;
Mature enough to be childlike;
Righteous enough to be a sinner;
Important enough to be last;
Courageous enough to fear God;
Planned enough to be spontaneous;
Controlled enough to be flexible;
Free enough to endure captivity;
Knowledgeable enough to ask questions;
Loving enough to be angry;
Great enough to be anonymous;
Responsible enough to play;

Assured enough to be rejected;
Stable enough to cry;
Victorious enough to relax;
Leading enough to serve.

A Little Blessing

May the time and labor you spend on
bringing about celebrations for all of God's
children give you:

> a little more awareness of their needs;
> a little more sense of belonging;
> a little chance for the children to claim ownership of the liturgy;
> a little bit of recognition of the presence of children;
> a little way to make liturgy come alive for all;
> a little better understanding of symbol and ritual in our liturgy;
> a little experience of hope;
> a little moment for all God's children to share their gifts; and
> a little taste of the kingdom of God.

Part One

A Little Love

1. The Gift of Love

Themes

- awareness of senior citizens or the lonely and elderly
- love for neighbor, love one another, God's love for us
- Valentine's Day

Scripture

- Mark 12:28-34
- John 13:31-35
- John 15:11-17

Setting

- living room

Props

- gift box on a table
- puppet stage if the puppets are used
- If done in a skit, the grandparents could have luggage upon arriving.

Characters

- Grandma
- Grandpa
- Boy
- Girl

Suggested Music

- "Love"
- "Grandma's House"

Suggested Handout

- wrapped "present"

BOY *is looking back and forth out the window.*

GIRL: (*Pacing back and forth*) Oh, I can hardly wait a minute longer. Are they here yet?

BOY: They should be here anytime now!

GIRL: They're here! Oh, they're finally here!

GRANDMA: (*Enters with* GRANDPA) Yes, we are finally here!

GRANDPA: My, my, how you've both grown!

GRANDMA: Let me take a good look at each one of you. Mmm, don't we have two of the most beautiful grandchildren ever!

BOY: We've missed you both so much. We have missed talking with you and sharing stories with you.

GIRL: We even told Mom and Dad that we missed you a lot and they came up with a great idea! They told us we could adopt a grandparent at this special place called a retirement center.

BOY: The center is not very far from here and we can go visit our adopted grandparent almost any time.

GRANDMA: Well, now that is good news! That is so kind of you to share your love with others. I wish more boys and girls would think of ways they could help people to not feel lonely.

GRANDPA: You know, kids, we older folks get real lonely and sometimes we feel like everyone's just too busy to take time to visit. Wouldn't it be wonderful if other kids adopted a grandparent, too? They could bring them a flower, or a home-made card, or chocolate chip cookies.

BOY: Oh, Grandpa, I bet it makes you feel sad to think of all the people who have no one to visit them.

GRANDPA: Sometimes! But if more of your friends would decide to visit retirement centers or nursing homes or hospitals, maybe we could *stop* loneliness.

GRANDMA: We need young people like you around to lift up our spirits!

GRANDPA: Each of you is a gift of hope and life to people like us. We are so lucky to have grandchildren like you.

GIRL: We love you so much and we wish you could just stay with us all the time.

BOY: Yeah, we have a lot of fun when we visit our adopted grandparents, but we do miss all those good stories you and Grandma share with us.

GRANDMA: We brought a special gift for you, and we had planned to give it to you when we leave for home next week. What do you think? (*She looks at* GRANDPA.) Should we give them our gift now?

GRANDPA: Absolutely. (*If the script is being used on Valentine's Day, add the following line:*) I think this is the perfect day to give them our gift of love. After all, Valentine's Day is a day to share love.

GIRL: (*Excitedly*) Oh, a gift for us?

GRANDMA: (*Showing them the little gift*) You have shown us so much love, we have this gift for you. It comes with a poem that tells you all about this present. Listen and I'll read it to you:

> This is a very special gift,
> Which you can never see.
> The reason it's so special is
> It's just for you from me.
> Whenever you are lonely,
> Or even feeling blue,
> You only have to hold this gift
> And know I think of you.
> You never can unwrap it,
> Please leave the ribbon tied.
> Just hold the box close to your heart.
> It's filled with love inside.

GRANDPA: You just take this little present and, when you start to miss us, you just hold this close to your heart and know we love you.

BOY: (*Somewhat disappointed*) Why can't we unwrap it?

GRANDMA: Because, dear, it is just a little reminder of our love. It's a symbol of our *gift* of love to you, not the real thing.

GIRL: So we can keep it in a special place in our room and when we feel sad or lonely because we miss you, we can hold it and just know we are loved.

BOY: Oh, it's a present full of love!

GRANDPA: That's right. Just like you two kids are full of love. You know, Grams, this gives me a great idea. Now when we go back to our home, maybe we ought to look into adopting a grandchild or two who may be lonely and missing their grandparents. If our grandkids can get involved to help others, maybe we should, too.

At this time the minister, priest, or the children's teachers hand out the gifts, telling the children that on this (Valentine's) day you give them a reminder of

God's everlasting love for them. This is a special gift. They should never unwrap it, but let it remind them that they should be gifts for others who might be lonely or need love.

Handout: "The Gift of Love"

Wrap square blocks (½-inch square) cut from scrap lumber in paper and ribbon in any color; photocopy poem below, then attach to present; use hole puncher to punch hole in paper with poem, then tie on with ribbon to present.

The Gift of Love

This is a very special gift,
Which you can never see.
The reason it's so special is
It's just for you from me.
Whenever you are lonely,
Or even feeling blue,
You only have to hold this gift
And know I think of you.
You never can unwrap it,
Please leave the ribbon tied.
Just hold the box close to your heart.
It's filled with love inside.

2. Happy Heartburn

Themes
- Jesus is with us.
- Our hearts are burning with love.

Scripture
- Luke 24:28-35

Setting
- kitchen or living room

Props
- glass of water
- Tums, Rolaids, or Pepto Bismol (obvious antacids)
- puppet stage if puppets are used

Characters
- Grandma
- Grandpa
- Boy
- Girl

Suggested Music
- "Are Not Our Hearts"
- "God Uses Kids"
- "Sing a Simple Song"
- "Smile!"
- "His Banner Over Us Is Love"
- "Our God Is a God of Love"

Suggested Handouts
- construction paper with pattern of four gingerbread girls and boys with happy heartburn (See Handout page.)
- heart-shaped candies (common around Valentine's Day)

GRANDPA: (*Singing alone*) Are not our hearts burning within us, Are not our hearts lighted with fire, Jesus is with us, is risen, is with us today....

> BOY *enters and watches* GRANDPA, *then leaves to find his sister.* GRANDPA *exits off.*

BOY: (*Calling his sister*) Come here quick! Something is wrong with Gramps!

GIRL: What? What's wrong with him?

BOY: I saw him standing in the other room, staring out the window. He had his hand on his heart and he was singing.

GIRL: So, what's the matter with that? He sings real good.

BOY: Well, I heard him singing about his heart burning within him.

GIRL: Oh, dear! Do you think he has heartburn? Oh, maybe it's his heart condition!

BOY: Let's call him in and see what's the matter. Gramps, where are you?

GRANDPA: (*Enters humming song.*) Right here! What do you need?

GIRL: Gramps, are you okay? Maybe you better come here and sit down and rest for a minute.

BOY: Can I get you a glass of water?

GIRL: How about some Tums or Rolaids?

GRANDPA: I'm perfectly fine, thank you!

BOY: Maybe you'd rather have some Pepto Bismol. Do you want me to get you some?

GRANDPA: Wait just a minute here! Now, why would I need all that medicine? I feel great!

GIRL: Gramps, you have to take care of yourself—especially with your condition. I can see you won't listen to us. I guess we had better get Grandma in here to help us.

BOY: Grandma, help, we have a problem in here. Come quick! Gramps won't take his medicine!

GRANDMA: What is going on in here? What's this about taking medicine?

BOY: Well, a little while ago I heard Gramps singing a song about how his heart was burning. He's got a bad case of the heartburn, and now he won't take his medicine!

GRANDPA: (*Laughing*) I don't have *that* kind of heartburn.

GIRL: Then what kind of heartburn do you have?

GRANDPA: My heart is just fine! It is just burning with love for Jesus! I'm singing because I'm happy.

GRANDMA: In the Good News story we heard today, two of Jesus' friends were walking along the road, and their hearts were burning with love for him. When your heart is so full of love, you just feel like singing and sharing that love with everyone around you.

GRANDPA: I just open my heart and let Jesus' love fill me up and, oh, how my heart burns with love!

BOY: Just listening to you talking about Jesus is making my heart burn with love, too.

GRANDMA: When you have Jesus' love inside your heart, it just sorta *has* to spill out.

GIRL: What happens to all that extra love spilling out?

GRANDMA: Well, you should take that love and share it with others.

BOY: When I grow up I'm gonna tell people about Jesus and all the special things God has done. I will tell them how my heart burns with love.

GRANDPA: Why wait till you are all grown up? You can start right now.

GIRL: But, Gramps, we are only kids. Nobody listens to kids.

GRANDPA: Well, kids are very special to God. God needs kids to spread love to all those around them.

GRANDMA: That's right! God uses kids to show others how to share love and joy. If you open up your hearts, God can use *you* today.

GRANDPA: I hope your hearts will always burn with love for Jesus. That's a *real* happy heartburn.

GRANDMA: Here's a song that tells the best remedy for all that happy heartburn.

Cast and audience may sing "God Uses Kids" or other suggested music with cassette accompaniment.

Handout: "Happy Heartburn"

Photocopy onto white paper and cut out. Students can tape or glue the cutouts onto construction paper slips, color them, and use as bookmarks.

3. Little Lights

Themes

- Jesus came to be our guide and show us the way.
- Jesus shows us how to love one another and let our light shine.

Scripture

- John 8:12-13
- 1 John 2:7-11

Setting

- on porch or outside

Props

- blindfold
- battery-operated candles (Christmas) that the children can pass around to each other

Characters

- Mom
- Dad
- Boy
- Girl

Suggested Music

- "Children of the Lord"
- "Follow Me"
- "This Little Light of Mine"

Suggested Handout

- construction-paper candles

GIRL: Did you see that man walking down the street?

BOY: You mean that man with that big dog?

GIRL: Yes. He was wearing dark glasses. Did you know that he is blind? He cannot see! That's why he has that dog to guide him.

BOY: Really? I wonder what it's like to be blind?

GIRL: Well, I'll show you. Come with me.

They exit off together and then come back with a blindfold over the boy's eyes.

BOY: Wow! I can't see anything! There's just a lot of darkness. I can't even see my hands.

GIRL: Now try to come over here where I am standing.

BOY: I can't. I hear your voice but I can't tell where you are.

GIRL: I'm over here. Can you find your way?

BOY: (Turns one way and bumps into something; turns the other way and bumps into something else.) I am lost! I can't find you! Please help me!

GIRL: Okay, I will help you. I will be your guide. Just take my hand and follow me. I'll show you the way. (*Takes his hand and leads him.*) Now, is that better?

BOY: Yes! This is much better!

MOM *and* DAD *enter together.*

DAD: What are you two up to?

GIRL: I am being a guide. He wanted to see what it was like to be blind but he needs a guide to find his way.

DAD: What does it feel like to be blind?

BOY: It's no fun at all! It's just awful! It's so dark in here. I don't like it. I want to be in the light. Can I take this off now? (Removes the blindfold.)

GIRL: Now you are in the light. Now you can see where you're going.

DAD: That's why blind people need a guide. They use a cane or a seeing-eye dog to help them.

MOM: Do you know that, even though you can see perfectly well, you have a guide, too?

GIRL: We don't need a guide. We aren't blind.

MOM: Jesus came to be our guide. He came to show us the way. Why don't you listen to our song and maybe it will help you to understand?

MOM *and* DAD *sing "Follow Me," and the* BOY *and* GIRL *join in.*

DAD: God sent Jesus into the world because He loves us so much. He sent Jesus to show us how to love one another. Jesus is the light of the world and when we follow him, then we are the children of light.

BOY: So, when I love and share with my family and friends, I am a child of the light? 'Cause I sure don't want to be in the dark!

MOM: That's right. Jesus' love just shines in you. When you share that love with friends who are sad or lonely, or hurt or afraid, they can see the light of Jesus in you.

DAD: When you let your light shine to friends, they will see the light in you and start to let their lights shine, and then they will pass the light on to others.

GIRL: Wouldn't it be a very bright and beautiful world if all of us let our lights shine?

BOY: I am going to let my light shine.

MOM: (*To audience*) Boys and girls, let's all sing "This Little Light of Mine" (*or other suggested music*).

As the children sing, the battery-operated candles are passed down each row so that all the children may hold them and then pass the candles on.

Handout: "Little Lights"

Cut out pattern, then use pattern to cut out construction-paper candles. Use felt pen to draw inside of flame and dripping wax.

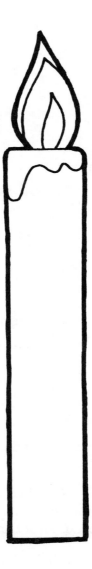

4. The Little Lost Lamb

Theme

- Parable of the Lost Sheep: Jesus loves us and cares about us. He is our shepherd; we are his sheep. We follow Jesus.

Scripture

- Matthew 18:10-14
- Luke 15:1-7

Setting

- Girl's room with lots of stuffed animals; then out in the dark, rainy night; then back to girl's room

Props

- a lamb
- lots of other stuffed animals on a shelf or bed
- a flashlight
- umbrella
- raincoats
- puppet stage if puppets are used

Sound Effects

- a tape recording of a storm
- a tin or metal sheet for thunder
- cellophane crumpled for rain

Characters

- Mom
- Dad
- Boy
- Girl
- Lovey Lamb (person in costume, or an offstage voice)

Suggested Music

- "The Lord Is My Shepherd"
- "Follow Me"
- "My Shepherd Is the Lord"
- "Psalm of the Good Shepherd"

Suggested Handouts

- a construction-paper lamb
- a lamb made from white sock (Use pink felt for ears, black ball fringe for eyes and nose.)

GIRL: Mommy, Daddy! Come quickly! I've lost my Lovey Lamb! I've looked everywhere in my room. I can't go to sleep without my Lovey. I just can't.

MOM: Well, dear, maybe if we look all around the house, we'll find her. Dad and I can help and we'll call your brother, too.

DAD: Son, come help us find your sister's lamb. She's lost it and she can't sleep without it.

BOY: Do I have to? She has a whole room full of animals. Can't she sleep with her teddy bear or one of her dolls?

MOM: (*Looking all around the room*) Well, we've looked everywhere, and Lovey is just not here. Where's the last place you saw Lovey?

GIRL: (*Thinking*) Oh, I remember. I was coming home from Sally's house and I was carrying my books, and my doll, and Lovey. Oh no! Do you think I might have dropped Lovey on the way home? Oh, no! Oh, can we go look for Lovey? Please? Please?

DAD: It's getting awfully dark, and a storm is coming. We'll have to hurry. Let's get going.

With flashlights and umbrellas, they go out into the night. Dim the lights if possible.

GIRL: Oh no! It's starting to rain. Poor Lovey will get all wet and cold. It's so dark. (*Starts to cry.*)

LOVEY: Baaa! Baaa! It's so scary out here. Baaa! It's so dark and I'm all alone. Baaa, Baaa! Help! Help! Oh, if only I could be home with my best friend, snuggling up in her warm bed. Baaa! Baaa!

Sound effects: thunder, rain and wind.

BOY: This is just ridiculous. I'm out here getting all wet. Is this really important? Can't we go back home? Why is Lovey so special?

GIRL: Look! Oh, look! I see Lovey. (*They all move over to the lamb.*) Oh, Lovey's all wet and scared. Oh, Lovey Lamb, I'm so glad we found you. We've been looking everywhere for you.

All return to the girl's room or living room.

MOM: Now, you can climb in bed and go to sleep, now that Lovey is back home with you.

DAD: Children, before you go to bed, I want to tell you a story. This is a story Jesus told many years ago. It's called a parable, the parable of the lost sheep. A shepherd had one hundred sheep—

BOY: That's just about how many animals and dolls you have right in this very room!

MOM: Shhh! Now, son, listen.

DAD: One night the shepherd gathered all his sheep into the gate, and as he counted them he saw that there were only ninety-nine sheep. He left these ninety-nine sheep and went out into the hills to search for the lost one. When he found it, he was so happy that he rejoiced over it more than over the ninety-nine others that were safe at home. This is the same way Jesus loves us and cares about us. Sometimes we're lost like the one sheep in Jesus' story.

GIRL: Like when we do something wrong or hurt someone?

DAD: Exactly!

MOM: And Jesus takes the time to find us and make sure that we are safe. It's because he loves us and cares for us. Just as you love and care about Lovey Lamb. Only Jesus loves us so much more!

DAD: Let's sing a song for everyone that will show what we mean.

All sing suggested song.

Handout: "The Little Lost Lamb"

Cut out pattern, then use pattern to cut sheep from white construction paper. With black felt pen draw *eye*, *ear*, and *mouth*, color legs, and write "Follow Me" on the front.

5. Love Forever

Themes

- God's love for us
- Deeper awareness of God's love
- Mother's Day

Scripture

- John 3:14-21

Setting

- Storytelling time, with children gathered around in the front of the worship center

Props

- a rocking chair or bench for the storyteller
- guitar
- bench
- storybook *Love You Forever*

Characters

- storyteller
- a choir member (to sing the verse from the story, may use a guitar to play the melody)

Suggested Music

- "His Banner Over Us Is Love"
- "Our God Is a God of Love"
- "Sing a Simple Song" ("Joey's Song")

Suggested Handout

- postcard

Presentation

The story *Love You Forever* is about a mother's unconditional love for her son. When we presented it, a young father in our community read the story. Each page tells of how the mother sings to her son, so a woman from the choir who played the guitar helped him write a melody to the song. When the lines of the story told of how the mother takes the child in her arms and sings, the woman, seated over by the choir, played the melody and sang the verse. At the end of the story, when the mother has grown so weak and old that she cannot finish the song, the son sings the song to her. After the mother dies, the son sings the song to his new baby daughter. At this point in our presentation, the reader sang the verse. The final verse was sung in harmony by both "mother" and "son."

Homily Idea

After the story, the homilist or priest can reflect on the unconditional love the mother has for her son. Then he or she can lead into how God's love is even greater than that love and how God loves each and every child. It may be a good way to draw the children into sharing by asking them how much they think God loves them, allowing them to show the "measure" of God's love with their hands.

Handout: "Love Forever"

Cut out the postcard pattern, then use pattern to cut construction-paper postcards. Copy the words and heart stamp onto each postcard.

FRONT

Child of God
(NAME OF CHURCH)
(CITY, STATE)

Dear Child,

I'll love you forever.

Love,
God

BACK

Part Two

A Little Thanks

6. A Little Giving, A Little Thanks

Themes

- Thanksgiving
- We can be thankful *every* day.
- We can give of ourselves *every* day.

Scripture

- Luke 17:11-19

Setting

- living room

Props

- decorations for Thanksgiving
- puppet stage if puppets are used

Characters

- Grandma
- Grandpa
- Mom
- Dad
- Boy
- Girl

Suggested Music

- "Be Thankful"
- "Thank You, God, for Being So Good"
- "Thank You, God"

Suggested Handout

- construction-paper cut cornucopias

DAD: You know, today is one of my favorite holidays. It's a day to give thanks.

BOY: It's one of my favorite times, too. All that good food. Mm! Mm!

GIRL: I like Thanksgiving because our family gets together.

MOM: I think we better go check on that turkey. Will you kids watch for your grandparents to arrive? They will be here any time now.

BOY: Okay, we'll watch.

   MOM *and* DAD *exit.*

GIRL: Oh, I can smell that turkey in here. Mmm!

BOY: I sure do hope grandma brings her famous pumpkin pie.

A knocking sound occurs offstage. GRANDMA *and* GRANDPA *enter.*

GRANDMA: Howdy, kids! Let me give my darlings a big hug.

GRANDPA: Oh, it sure smells good in here. Happy Thanksgiving! Where are your Mom and Dad?

GIRL: They are checking on the turkey.

BOY: Grandpa, don't you just love Thanksgiving? We get to eat, and eat, and stuff ourselves with all that good food!

GRANDPA: There's always good food on Thanksgiving, but do you know there's more to this day then just eating?

GIRL: Sure. It's a day we give thanks.

BOY: We thank God for all our blessings.

GRANDMA: Yes, that's right. And we sure have lots of blessings.

GRANDPA: I like to celebrate Thanksgiving every day!

BOY: You mean you eat turkey every day?

GIRL: Every day?

GRANDPA: No, I don't mean I eat turkey every day. I mean that *every day* I like to give thanks to God. Then, I ask myself if I remembered to thank all the people who helped me and shared love with me that day.

GIRL: Gee, I guess I forget to do that every day.

BOY: I kinda forget to thank God every day, too.

GRANDMA: In the story from the gospel, the ten lepers were cured and only one of them came back to thank Jesus. I think this story is a good reminder for us. We need to thank God and everyone who helps us each day.

GRANDPA: And don't forget the rest of the word, "giving." Giving of yourself is very important, too.

GIRL: Oh, I get it. Every day we need to give a little thanks and a little giving. Like when I give my grandma a big hug and say thank you for making your famous pumpkin pie.

BOY: Yeah, I'm very thankful I can help Grandpa carry in those pumpkin pies. Come on, Gramps, let's go get them.

Music from cassette is played, or choir sings song.

Handout: "A Little Giving, A Little Thanks"

Cut out the cornucopia pattern, then use the pattern to make construction-paper cornucopias. Copy the words as shown.

7. Sharing Brings True Riches

Themes

- Sharing our blessings with others
- All we have comes from God.

Scripture

- Mark 10:17-31
- Luke 12:16-21

Setting

- kitchen or living room

Props

- pennies
- a few glass jars
- puppet stage if puppets are used

Characters

- Grandma
- Grandpa
- Boy
- Girl

Suggested Music

- "I Am Only One"
- "We Come to Share"
- "Sharing Comes Round Again"

Suggested Handouts

- construction-paper piggy banks
- construction-paper bread loaves

BOY: (Counting his pennies from jars of pennies beside him) 3002, 3003, 3004. I sure have a lot of pennies.

GIRL: (Entering) Are you still counting your pennies?

BOY: Yes, I am. Will you just look at all these jars? I have so many pennies that I'm running out of jars! Do you want to help me count them?

GIRL: You sure do have a lot. What are you going to do with all that money?

BOY: I am so rich! I can buy a lot of toys or just about anything I want.

GIRL: (Somewhat frustrated) Oh, I am going to the park to play. I'm getting real tired of hearing about all your money. You are a real penny pincher. (Leaves stage.)

GRANDMA and GRANDPA: (*Entering*) Hello! Hello!

BOY: Oh, hi!

GRANDMA: Ooh! Let me give my grandson a big hug. Hasn't he grown since we saw him last?

GRANDPA: He sure has!

BOY: Now be very careful; don't knock over my penny jars. I'm just too busy for hugs today. I'm real busy counting all my pennies.

GRANDPA: (*Looks over at* GRANDMA *and scratches his head.*) Oh, too busy for hugs, eh?

GRANDMA: I sure hope you aren't too busy to help me start baking all the pies and breads for Thanksgiving Day. We only have a few days to get ready for our feast.

BOY: Well, I'll have to see about that! I don't know if I'll be finished counting all my pennies by then.

GIRL: (*Enters wiping her eyes and upset; sees her grandparents and goes over to give them a hug.*) Oh, I'm so glad you are both here.

GRANDPA: Is something wrong? You look as if you are crying!

GIRL: I have been. I was just at the park and I talked with a little girl there. She told me that her family won't be having turkey on Thanksgiving. Can you believe it? They don't have any money to buy a turkey.

GRANDMA: Oh, dear, that's just awful. (*Shakes her head.*)

BOY: Well, you think that's awful, just look here. I don't have any more jars for my pennies. What should I do?

GIRL: We have to do something to help this family! (*Pauses for a moment to think.*) I know. I have a great idea! We could all pitch in some money and buy them everything they would need for a turkey dinner. How about it?

BOY: Not me. I'm going to buy some toys and games just for me.

GIRL: We weren't going to even ask you! (*Puts her hands on her hips and says with contempt:*) A penny pincher wouldn't give any way!

GRANDPA: Now children, do you know that everything we have is a gift from God? We ought to share our gifts with each other.

GRANDMA: Darlin', your pennies may make you feel rich, but sharing them brings you many more riches and blessings.

BOY: Is having money wrong?

GRANDPA: Money is a gift from God, but when it becomes more important than God, or when we don't share it with others, then something is sure wrong.

GIRL: Come on, Grandma. I've got some money and you and gramps do, too. Let's count it up and see what we've got. (*Looks over to her brother.*) Well, are you going to join us? Are you going to pitch in some of your pennies or are you going to be a penny pincher all your life?

BOY: Oh, all right. Here's my share. I will empty two whole jars of my pennies. Everyone should be able to have a turkey dinner on Thanksgiving. Gramps, let's go buy that turkey.

GRANDPA: That sounds like a great idea.

BOY: You know what? Sharing my pennies doesn't make me feel so bad. In fact, it makes me feel richer. And now I won't need to find any more jars—at least for a while.

ALL: Happy Thanksgiving to all of you. We have a special gift for you to take home and put on your table. When you are all together at the table, maybe you and your family can talk about sharing.

Handout #1: "Sharing Brings True Riches"

Cut out piggy bank pattern, then use pattern to make piggy banks from white or pink construction paper. With felt pen, copy eye, slot, and words as shown.

Handout #2: "Sharing Brings True Riches"

Cut out bread loaf pattern, then use pattern to make construction-paper bread loaves. Copy words as shown. Fold in half to stand up on families' tables.

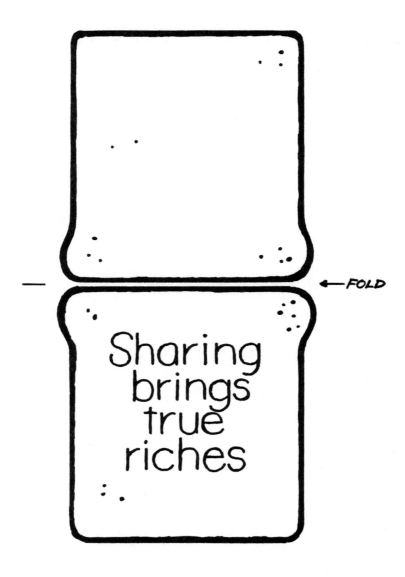

← *FOLD*

Sharing brings true riches

Part Three

A Little Justice

8. Heart to Change the World

Themes

- If we change our hearts, we can change the world.
- Love your enemies.

Scripture

- Luke 6:27-36

Setting

- outside on steps or on porch

Props

- puppet stage if puppets are used

Characters

- Mom
- Dad
- Boy
- Girl

Suggested Music

- "Heart to Change the World"
- "Jesu, Jesu Fill Us with Your Love"
- "Peace Prayer"
- "Peace Time"

Suggested Handouts

- two construction-paper heart-shaped balloons
- two real balloons with inscriptions printed with permanent, fine line marker (For safety's sake, and just because, this handout should be given after the celebration is over and the children are leaving.)

BOY: (*Running up to his parents*) Have we got problems! Dad, we want to move to a new neighborhood! We've had it with this place!

GIRL: Yeah! All the kids are yelling and screaming. They are all fighting and wanting their own way!

DAD: Sounds like you do have a big problem.

MOM: What do you think you can do about all the fighting?

GIRL: (*Snobbishly*) We could tell the ones who won't stop fighting that we will never play with them again. That would show them!

BOY: Or, we could scream and holler till we get our way! Maybe we should just give them a fist sandwich. (*Makes a fist with his hand and then punches an imaginary person.*)

DAD: Well, do you think any of those ideas will solve the problem?

GIRL: Not really.

BOY: Probably not.

MOM: Do you kids know that sometimes adults behave the same way as the kids in our neighborhood do? It happens with leaders of countries and in places where people work. When we all want our own way, we sometimes don't care who we hurt to get what we want. And do you know that many wars have started just for that very reason?

DAD: I wonder what would happen if everyone had a change of heart, beginning with each one in this family?

GIRL: Change of heart? What's that?

DAD: That's a heart full of love that shares with others, rather than a heart filled with *me, me, me!*

BOY: But that means they would get their way! That's not fair! I want to get my way, too! (Stamps his foot on the ground in protest.)

GIRL: Well, I guess we could take turns.

BOY: (*Hesitantly*) I guess so. It is really only fair if we all take turns.

MOM: That's a great idea. If we can share, we can let our friends see that we are peacemakers for Jesus. And if we can stop the "little wars" in our own neighborhood, then we can help change the world, a little tiny piece at a time.

BOY: Change the world? Mom, it's only the kids down the street we're talkin' about!

MOM: Peace can spread from "kids down the street" to neighborhoods, to cities, to countries. When we change our hearts and show love and treat others with respect, we can help change the world!

DAD: Your mom is absolutely right! The words to one of my favorite songs say it best.

Play "Heart to Change the World" cassette. When the song is over, DAD *stands up and listens carefully. Then he looks at the children.*

DAD: I think I hear some kids calling for you two. Go on now and make peace in this little corner of the world.

Handout: "Heart to Change the World"

Cut out balloons pattern, then use pattern to make construction-paper balloons. Copy words as shown.

9. It Starts with a Heart Full of Love

Themes

- RENEW
- social justice
- sharing and caring

Scripture

- Matthew 25:31-46
- Luke 6:20-26

Setting

- Living room or kitchen

Props

- chairs or a bench around a table
- popcorn
- puppet stage if puppets are used

Characters

- Boy
- Girl
- Grandma
- Grandpa

Suggested Music

- "Heart to Change the World"
- "What We Need in This World Is"
- "Service"
- "Reach Out"

Suggested Handout

- construction-paper cross with a heart in the middle

GRANDPA *and* GRANDMA *are sitting together talking.*
BOY *and* GIRL *enter and exchange hellos and hugs.*

GIRL: We're so happy that you are staying with us tonight. Oh, can we fix some popcorn?

BOY: Yeah, we always have so much fun when you are here.

GIRL: By the way, just where did Mom and Dad go?

GRANDMA: They went to a RENEW meeting tonight.

BOY: RENEW, RENEW, RENEW, that's all we've been hearing about lately. What's that all about?

GRANDPA: All of the Catholic communities in our area have been meeting together in small groups to share their stories and their faith.

GRANDMA: They all meet once a week to learn more about Jesus. It helps all of us to become more caring and loving people.

GIRL: Well, what kind of stories do they share?

GRANDPA: One of the topics we discussed was social justice.

BOY *and* GIRL *look very puzzled.*

BOY: Whoa, Gramps, you're talking way over my head.

GIRL: Could you please put that into kid's talk? I just don't even know what that means.

GRANDMA: Social justice is when the people in our families, neighborhoods, and cities are treated fairly.

GRANDPA: We are in a RENEW group, too. We talk about how we can open our eyes and our ears and our hearts and start caring for those people around us who need help, those people who have not been treated justly.

GRANDMA: Some of the people in our group share their stories about how they haven't been treated fairly. We all listen, and then we talk about what we can do to make life better for them and for all people.

BOY: Why can't people be fair to each other?

GIRL: I think a lot of people have forgotten how to share.

GRANDPA: That's for sure! There are many ways we can share with others. Your grandma and I decided to go downtown to the soup kitchen once a week and help serve food to the hungry people in our city.

BOY: Why do they call it a soup kitchen?

GRANDMA: A soup kitchen is a place where people can come to eat every day when they have no money to buy food.

GIRL: You mean they can't even feed their children supper? Oh, that is a sad story. It gets me right here in the heart.

GRANDMA: Yes, people are treated unfairly because people don't use their hearts when dealing with each other.

GRANDPA: Yes, that is where it all starts!

BOY: In the heart?

GRANDMA: Yes indeed! When we have love in our hearts, that is when we can start to care. When we care, the sharing can begin.

GRANDPA: When we love from the heart, and the sharing begins, then we show Jesus' love to everyone.

GRANDMA: That is one way we can help put an end to social injustice; that is how we can help change the world.

If there is time, the characters could enter into a dialogue with those present at the liturgy, especially the children, asking how they might get involved in creating a just society where they are: on a little league team, at a Girl Scout meeting, in their classrooms, with their families, after school, on the bus, etc. At the conclusion, those present can sing "Heart to Change the World" or another selection from the suggested music.

Handout: "It Starts with a Heart Full of Love"

Cut out pattern, then use pattern to make construction-paper cross with heart. Outline heart in red felt pen and cross in brown, then print the words in the heart.

10. Rainbow Children

Themes

- world peace
- one body of Christ
- all sisters and brothers in this world
- environmental awareness

Setting

- liturgy

Props

- large plastic world globe ball and table to display it on
- votive candles to encircle globe
- banners or flags from different countries
- costumes from different countries

Characters

- priest, deacon, or homilist
- children from different countries (United States, Vietnam, Central America, South America, Spain, Portugal, China, Africa, Germany, Ireland, Japan, Poland, Britain, Italy, Israel, Russia, etc.). Hopefully, you may be able to find some of these children within your own community. It would be even better if children could speak in their native languages.

Suggested Music

- "The World Is a Rainbow"
- "Dona Nobis Pacem"
- "Let There Be Peace on Earth"
- "The Peace of the Lord"
- "Peace Time"
- Other world peace songs can be found in hymnals, popular music, and children's music books.

Suggested Handout

- construction-paper world with children's faces

Presentation and Homily Idea

The children can share a greeting in their own language or share a little about their culture. The homilist can talk about how each one is different, but we are all the family of God, brothers and sisters. Discuss how we can bring peace to our world when we can all join hands together. At this time the children in the cast can light the candles and do a simple dance around the globe to a peace song. Depending on your selection of music, simple gestures can be taught to the children watching, so that they can join in also. The children can then read a prayer for world peace and unity.

This presentation could also be used for a prayer service with children. This could include a discussion on pollution, waste or recycling if done in a classroom setting or on a retreat. If you use the song "Dona Nobis Pacem" ("Grant Us Peace"), the children can easily pick up the words and sing in rounds. You might want to tell the children what the Latin words mean. It is a good song for dancing around the globe.

Handout: "Rainbow Children"

Cut out circle shape, then use as pattern to cut worlds out of light blue construction paper. In black felt pen, copy continents and faces. Children may take these home and color.

11. Sharing Our Silver Spoons

Themes
- talents and gifts God gave us to share
- sharing what we have in thanksgiving to God

Scripture
- Mark 10:17-30

Props
- jewelry
- fancy clothes
- fur coat
- silver spoon

Characters
- Reader to narrate story
- Chorus (one or more persons)
- Woman
- musician to accompany chorus with background music, such as guitar

Suggested Music
- "Sharing Comes Round Again, Give It Away"
- "Love That Is Kept Inside"
- "We Come to Share"
- "We Are Many Parts"
- any song about sharing

Suggested Handouts
- construction-paper silver spoons
- plastic silver spoons (may be found at a party store)

READER: Once upon a time,

CHORUS: Once upon a time,

READER: There was born a beautiful baby with a silver spoon in her mouth.

CHORUS: A silver spoon in her mouth.

READER: As she grew older she realized that she could have anything she wanted.

CHORUS: Servants, fine clothes, jewels, cars.

READER: She married a fine man who had also been born with a silver spoon in his mouth.

CHORUS: Anything he wanted.

READER: Soon children were born to them and they were born—

CHORUS: Yes, we know, with silver spoons in their mouths.

> WOMAN, *with silver spoon in her mouth and wearing fancy clothes and/or fur coat and jewelry, enters.*

READER: Anyway, one day the Lord appeared to the woman and asked, "Are you having a good life?"

WOMAN: Yes.

READER: Said the woman.

WOMAN: Very nice.

READER: "Well," said the Lord, "I thought I would have heard from you by now."

> WOMAN *looks around to see if the Lord is talking to someone else and then, seeing no one, she answers,*

WOMAN: Do I know you?

READER: "Well," said the Lord, "we did meet years ago, but you seem to have forgotten me."

CHORUS: The woman looked at the Lord blankly. She had no idea where they had met.

READER: The Lord continued: "What you have—all of your blessings, your material wealth as well as your family and friends, your beautiful lifestyle, the trees, the flowers, the food you eat—all come from me."

WOMAN: Oh, no!

CHORUS: Said the woman.

WOMAN: I was born with a silver spoon in my mouth. You gave me nothing.

READER: "Nothing?" asked the Lord.

WOMAN: Nothing.

CHORUS: Nothing!

READER: "I thought," said the Lord, "that since you have so much you might be thankful and in your gratitude you might want to share with others."

WOMAN: Oh, I see. Well, if you are a beggar, you may go to the back door and the cook will give you a piece of food.

CHORUS: If you chop the wood!

READER: "I am not a beggar," said the Lord. "I am a king."

WOMAN: Oh, well. Kings may go in the front door.

CHORUS: Oh, yes, please, the front door.

WOMAN: But, if you are a king, why are you asking for a handout?

READER: "It's not for me," said the king. "It's for your sisters and brothers."

WOMAN: Now I know you mistake me. I have no sisters and brothers.

READER: "Oh yes," said the Lord. "You have a world full of them."

WOMAN: You mean I am to feed the world?

READER: "Feed my sheep!"

WOMAN: But what do you mean?

READER: "You know what I mean," said the Lord. "To those who are given much, from them much is required."

CHORUS: Much is required!

READER: And what happened to the woman who was born with a silver spoon in her mouth?

CHORUS: She did know what the Lord meant.

READER: And now she takes her silver spoon and feeds her hungry brothers and sisters.

CHORUS: What do you mean?

READER: You know what I mean.

WOMAN *pretends she is feeding the children with her silver spoon.**

---

* Adapted from *Silver Spoons: Reaching for Rainbows* by Ann Weems (Philadelphia: Westminster Press, 1980).

Homily Idea

After the skit, your minister or other adult could talk to the children about sharing their gifts and how all of us are born with silver spoons (or special gifts) and how we can share them. As the children are returning to their seats, give each a silver spoon to take home and share with their families the gifts they have and how they can share them.

While the spoons are being distributed, the choir or soloist can sing a song from the suggested music.

Handout: "Sharing Our Silver Spoons"

Cut out spoon pattern, then use pattern to make "silver" spoons out of grey construction paper. Write "Share" as shown.

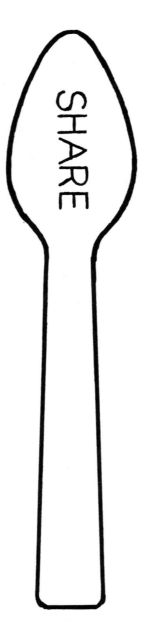

Part Four

A Little Wholiness

12. The Best I Can Do

Themes

- becoming whole
- saints in the making

Scripture

- Matthew 5:1-12
- 1 John 3:1-3

Setting

- walking home from school, then the kitchen

Props

- backpack or schoolbooks
- puppet stage if puppets are used

Sound Effect

- door slamming

Characters

- Girl
- Friend
- Boy
- Mother

Suggested Music

- "He's Still Working on Me, You've Got to Try"
- "Color the World with Song"
- "Abba! Father!"
- "Sing a Simple Song"

Suggested Handout

- construction-paper award ribbon

GIRL *is walking home from school with her* FRIEND.

FRIEND: Aren't you coming over to my house?

GIRL: No, not today! I have to get my homework done.

FRIEND: Right now? You always come over on Tuesday after school so we can practice our dance routine! Did you forget?

GIRL: No, I just can't come over today. I have to finish my homework. I am joining the choir at our church and our first practice is tonight. This is something I have always wanted to do. I'm really excited!

FRIEND: Oh, I see. Choir.

GIRL: Maybe I should start warming up as I walk. (*Sings the scale.*) La, la, la, la, la, la, la, la.

FRIEND: (*Giggling*) Oh really! Do you think they will let you in the choir with a voice like that? You gotta be kidding! You sound kinda squeaky to me.

GIRL looks at her friend and slowly bows her head. Then, hurt, she walks away.

FRIEND: See ya! I'm going to go practice my dance. (Exits off.)

GIRL, head hung down, walks off stage. The scene switches to the house. The BOY and his MOTHER are in the kitchen talking. They are startled when they hear the door slam.

BOY: (*Jumps as if startled*) What was that?

GIRL enters.

MOM: Hi, how was your day?

GIRL: (*Angrily*) My day was *just fine.*

BOY: Oh, really? Then what's wrong?

GIRL: (*Getting madder*) There is nothing wrong!

MOM: Let's get going on your homework, so we can get to choir practice tonight.

BOY: Oh, yeah, that's tonight.

GIRL: I have plenty of time to do my homework 'cause I am *not* going to choir. I'll be in my room. (*Starts to leave.*)

MOM: Hold on a minute! Are you sure there's nothing bothering you?

BOY: Sure does sound like something is wrong. Oh, she's stuffing her feelings down inside.

MOM: I thought you wanted to be in the choir. You were looking forward to it.

GIRL: Why would I want to be in the choir? I can't even carry a tune!

MOM: How do you know that you can't carry a tune until you've tried?

GIRL: I have tried. I sound awful!

BOY: I've heard you sing. I think you have a good voice.

GIRL: No, someone told me I was squeaky!

MOM: And who might that someone be?

GIRL: My friend.

MOM: Why would a friend say that? Sounds like your friend has hurt your feelings. Do you want to talk about it?

GIRL: (*Shakes her head.*) No.

MOM: Sometimes when we share big hurts, they can become smaller hurts. They get smaller and smaller till they just go away. Sharing our pain and hurts can heal us and help us.

GIRL: Oh, all right. I'll tell you what happened. My friend and I were walking home from school, and I was practicing my singing. She laughed at me and told me they would never let me in the choir with my squeaky voice.

BOY: Oh, I would have been mad!

MOM: How did you feel when she said that?

GIRL: I felt real sad. I couldn't believe she would say that to me. I almost started to cry.

MOM: Let's think for just a minute. Why do you think she would say that to you?

BOY: I bet she is jealous because she's not in the choir.

GIRL: No, she doesn't want to be in the choir. She just likes to be in our dance class, and all she ever wants to do is practice.

BOY: Isn't this the night you two always practice for dance?

GIRL: Yes, why?

BOY: Don't you see? She's upset because you're going to choir practice and not spending time with her.

GIRL: You're right. She's mad 'cause I wasn't coming over to practice with her.

MOM: You see why she said that about your singing? She's afraid that you won't want to practice dance with her any more.

GIRL: But, I'm not very good at singing either.

MOM: Singing takes lots of practice. Anything we really want to do, we have to work hard at and give our best shot. It takes a whole life time to discover what God wants us to be and to try to become that person.

GIRL: I don't know. Maybe I should forget about choir and stick to dancing.

MOM: This is what becoming whole or holy means. The saints that we read about weren't perfect at everything they did, but they kept trying. They always tried to do their best.

BOY: We learned about the disciples, the friends that Jesus asked to follow him. Some of them were just ordinary fishermen and people. They had so much to learn about building a church.

MOM: So, are you feeling any better about trying out for choir?

GIRL: Much better now. I don't feel as sad as I did. I feel relieved that I shared my hurt with you. If I hadn't talked it out with you, I might have stuffed all my hurt inside.

BOY: When someone hurts our feelings or makes fun of us, it can sometimes stop us from becoming what God wants us to be.

GIRL: I may sound a little squeaky, but I'm going to go to choir tonight and try. I'll give it my very best.

MOM: Now that's music to my ears! All you can *ever* do is to try to do your very best. Jesus will take care of the rest.

BOY: How about we do a little practicing right now?

Everyone sings "You've Got to Try" or other suggested music.

Handout: "The Best I Can Do"

Cut out pattern, then use pattern to make construction-paper award ribbons.

13. Fingerprints

Theme

- Fingerprints are special when they reach out and touch other people's lives.

Scripture

- Matthew 8:1-4; 8:14-17; 9:18-26; 9:27-31
- any passage where Jesus touches someone to heal him or her

Note: If you use Scripture other than Matthew 8:1-4, make appropriate changes to MOM's *line about Peter's mother-in-law.*

Setting

- living room or kitchen, by a wall with fingerprints

Props

- Before the liturgy begins, copies of fingerprints can be taped at various places throughout the worship center to arouse the curiosity of the assembly before the skit begins. These can be done the week before by the children in their religion classes.

Characters

- Boy
- Girl
- Mom
- Dad

Suggested Music

- "Fingerprints"
- "Reach Out"

Suggested Handout

- construction-paper handprint

MOM *enters and looks at the wall covered with finger-prints.*

MOM: What is all this? Everywhere I look there are more fingerprints! I know I already cleaned this wall once today. I can't believe my eyes; the fingerprints are back!

BOY *and* GIRL *enter with* DAD *close behind them.*

BOY: Hi, Mom! What is the matter?

GIRL: Uh-oh, are you upset?

MOM: Look, they are everywhere! These fingerprints are all over here, all over there. Now, I just want to know to whom do they belong?

GIRL: (Looks at the wall) Not me.

BOY: (*Looks at the wall and shrugs his shoulders*) I don't know.

GIRL: Maybe they are Dad's.

DAD: Do you kids know that *every* one of us has our very own special fingerprints? And no two are exactly alike!

MOM: In fact, I can see two different sets of fingerprints right here on this wall.

GIRL: Can you tell, just by looking, who they belong to?

MOM: Hmmm. (*Looking closely at prints*) It seems to me that they must belong to someone who is just about your size.

GIRL: (*Bites her hand and looks scared.*) Uh-oh.

DAD: Fingerprints are special, but they don't belong on the walls.

BOY: Well, where do they belong?

GIRL: Oh, I know! We can make pretty pictures on paper with our fingerprints.

BOY: Yeah, but we get into trouble if we put them anywhere else.

DAD: No, there are a lot of ways we can use our fingerprints.

MOM: We can use them to reach out and touch those around us who may need our help. We can use them to touch people's lives.

DAD: In the Good News today we heard a story about Jesus using his fingerprints.

If using Scripture other than Matthew 8:1-4, make appropriate changes to the following line.

MOM: Yes. Jesus touched Peter's mother-in-law, who was very sick. He reached out and took her by the hand and his loving touch helped her to feel better.

BOY: But Jesus was all grown up; we are still kind of small.

GIRL: (Bashfully) Sometimes I am afraid to reach out and touch others. I get shy.

BOY: That's taking a big chance, isn't it?

DAD: It certainly is, but it is a chance worth taking. When we touch others by loving them and caring about them, we feel really good inside.

BOY: Well, now we understand a lot more about fingerprints. They are how we touch others, how we reach out to care.

GIRL: (*Nodding her head*) Maybe if we sing this song for you, then our fingerprints will touch your lives!

BOY *and* GIRL *sing song.*

Handout: "Fingerprints"

Cut out pattern, then use pattern to make construction-paper handprints. Copy words as shown. If you decide to post the handprints in your worship space before liturgy, use class time for children to draw in their fingerprints and print the words.

Reach out and touch someone's Life

14. Not Quite Finished Yet

Themes

- God is still working on us.
- We're under construction and we're not quite finished.
- We make mistakes and we are still learning and growing.

Scripture

- Mark 4:26-29
- Mark 10:13-16

Setting

- porch, front step, or living room

Props

- shirt splattered with paint
- tools
- "Under Construction" signs
- puppet stage if puppets are used

Characters

- Boy
- Girl
- Grandpa
- Grandma

Suggested Music

- "Kids Under Construction"
- "May We Grow"

Suggested Handout

- "Under Construction" sign

BOY and GIRL enter stage hurriedly.

BOY: Oh, no! I think we're in big trouble this time.

GIRL: You've got paint all over your shirt, and now we've got the neighbor next door upset. What a mess!

BOY: (*Covers his face and shakes his head.*) What a *big mess*! What do we do now?

GIRL: (*Nudges the* BOY) Uh, oh! Here come Grandma and Grandpa.

GRANDMA *and* GRANDPA *enter.*

GRANDMA: Hi kids. We just stopped by to see how you were doing. Did I hear you say something about a big mess?

GRANDPA: I have this funny feeling that something is going on around here. Do you want to tell us about it?

GIRL: Well, we were over at the neighbor's and...I guess...we kinda got in his way. He's very upset!

BOY: It's even worse than that! I knocked over his can of paint, and just look at me.

GIRL: He's building something, and we were asking him a lot of questions. We were just wondering what he was doing.

BOY: He got real mad when she (*pointing at* GIRL) tried to saw some wood.

GIRL: I was only trying to help.

BOY: He told her she talked too loud, and then he asked if we'd left our manners at home.

GIRL: I was only kidding when I asked him if he had gotten up on the wrong side of the bed!

BOY: He sure didn't think that was very funny.

GRANDMA: Oh dear. Well! We older folks sometimes forget what it was like to be kids.

GRANDPA: When I was your age, many years ago, I was always exploring and discovering how things worked. I loved to build things and I learned so much. Once I even took apart my dad's radio so I could see how it was made.

BOY: You did? Wow, I bet your dad was mad!

GRANDPA: No. My dad just sat me down and this is what he told me. He said: "Son, I know that at your age you want to learn and discover all that you can. And sometimes you can get in a bit of trouble along the way. You need to be just a little more patient. Just slow down a bit. You know that God made you, and God loves you. You're just not quite finished yet."

GRANDMA: Children, it's the same for you. God is still working on you.

GIRL: Oh, I get it. It's like we are under construction.

GRANDMA: Now you got it, honey!

BOY: (*Looking down at his shirt*) And sometimes the paint is still a little wet!

BOY *and* GIRL *giggle together.*

GRANDMA: Let's sing a song for all God's children who are not quite finished yet!

All sing selected song.

Handout: "Not Quite Finished Yet"

Cut out the pattern, then use the pattern to make construction-paper signs. Use felt pen to outline and print words.

Part Five

A Little Sharing

15. Body Building

Themes

- body of Christ
- spiritual gifts

Scripture

- 1 Corinthians 2:12-30

Setting

- liturgy

Props

- large posterboard cut in a big gingerbread body pattern
- Optional: barbells and/or other exercise equipment placed around area where children will come up to sit

Characters

- priest, deacon, or homilist

Suggested Music

- "We Are Many Parts"
- "Welcome to the Family"

Suggested Handout

- a crayon and a construction-paper gingerbread body (Give these out as children enter for liturgy.)

Presentation/Homily Idea

Leader invites the children to come up, bringing their handouts and crayons with them. Leader invites them to print their names on the body shapes. For younger children, Mom or Dad will have to help.

The homilist talks to the children while they work, explaining the reading from 1 Corinthians 12:12-30. Include how we all belong to the body of Christ and that each member has special gifts.

Then ask the children to come up row by row (or five at a time) and pin their body shapes on the large body. A helper can stand near the large body to hand the children pins and collect crayons. Music from the choir or a cassette can be played at this time.

Next, reread the Scripture from 1 Corinthians, or let a few of the children read it. Afterward, the homilist can talk about how we build up our physical bodies by exercising with weights. We build up the body of Christ when we use all our gifts and talents (our sharing, caring and love) to strengthen the community.

After liturgy, display the body of Christ montagé created by the children in the foyer of the worship center or in the entry near the classrooms.

Handout: "Body Building"

Copy the body shape onto a large piece of posterboard or cardboard for display in the worship space. Then cut out the body pattern and make construction-paper body shapes to hand out to the children as they arrive for liturgy.

16. Pass the Peace, Please!

Theme

- Jesus gives us the gift of peace, and we share it with those around us.

Scripture

- John 14:25-31
- John 20:19-31
- Galatians 5:22-23

Setting

- living room

Props

- puppet stage if puppets are used
- pajamas for Boy and Girl if acted out

Characters

- Mom
- Boy
- Girl

Suggested Music

- "Peace"
- "Peace Prayer"
- "Peace Time"
- "The Peace of the Lord"
- "Peace Is Flowing Like a River"

Suggested Handout

- paper hands

GIRL: (*All ready for bed with pajamas on*) Mommy, could I maybe sleep on the floor in your room tonight?

MOM: Oh, I don't think so.

BOY: She's just being a scaredy cat. (*Taunting his sister*) She's afraid the boogey man's gonna get her!

GIRL: Not!

MOM: What's the matter? Are you afraid?

GIRL: I just don't want to sleep in my room all alone. I wish I had a sister or someone to sleep in my room with me.

BOY: You are such a big baby!

GIRL: No, I am not. I just don't want to be alone.

BOY: Well, you should be brave like me. I am going to bed right now. I'm not a fraidy cat. *(Gives* MOM *a hug and kiss.)* Goodnight, Mom. *(As he walks by his sister, he makes noises like a ghost.)* Wooo-ooo!

MOM: Wait a minute, son. Don't tease; you are hurting her feelings. We should help each other. When people are having a hard time, they need to talk about it. They don't need someone trying to make them feel worse. Goodnight now. See you in the morning.

MOM: *(Motions to* GIRL*)* Come here! Let's talk about what's bothering you.

GIRL: Well, Mom, sometimes I just get a little lonely in my room all by myself. I know you are not far away, but I sure feel all alone.

MOM: Oh, I see. You are feeling lonely. You know, this reminds me of what we heard today while we were at church. Do you remember? Jesus left us with—

BOY: *(Running in, calling)* Mom, Mom, I think I want to stay up a while with you. Uh, can I sit by you, too?

MOM: Has something scared you, son? You look like you've just seen a ghost!

BOY: *(In a frightened voice)* No, I'm not scared.

GIRL: Then why are you shaking? I think you are the scaredy cat now.

BOY: I am not. It's just that my nightlight went out in my room. I don't know who turned it out.

GIRL: *(Mocking her brother's earlier taunt of her)* Wooo-ooo!

MOM: Okay, let's stop all this spooky stuff. I think that probably your nightlight bulb must have burnt out. No one came in there and turned it out. We'll get another bulb and fix it in a minute.

BOY: Whew! Well, I guess I did get just a little scared for a minute there.

MOM: I was just saying that in church today we heard the Good News that Jesus left us a special gift. His friends were upset because he told them he would be leaving them soon. He was going to be with his Father in heaven. They were so very afraid to be left alone. He told them not to let their hearts be troubled, not to be afraid. He promised them that he would leave them with a special gift, the gift of peace.

BOY: Gift of peace? What kind of gift is that?

MOM: It's a wonderful gift: peace of mind and heart. It's having a calm feeling inside that lets you know that everything will be okay. It's a safe kind of feeling. And Jesus meant us to share with each other the peace that he gave us. We do that when we love each other, when we forgive each other, and when we—

BOY: Oh, and when we help each other, too.

MOM: That's right. Peace is holding onto Jesus with one hand and reaching out your other hand to share that peace with others. How about I show you what I mean? (*Gives her daughter a big hug.*)

BOY: (*Looking at the two of them with a puzzled expression*) What are you two doing? Tell me. What's going on now?

MOM: We are passing God's peace to each other.

GIRL: Yeah, we are passing the peace. Would you like some?

BOY: Yes. Could I have some of God's peace, too? Pass the peace, please!

GIRL: We just have to remember that when we are lonely or afraid, all we have to do is pass God's special gift of peace to each other and remind each other that God loves us and cares for us and will help us to stop being afraid.

All exchange hugs with each other.

MOM: Now that you have God's peace, let's get you both to bed!

BOY and GIRL: (*Turning toward the assembly*) Let's all pass the peace to each other, and to all the people we meet today.

All exchange hugs or handshakes with those around them. Music is played as the children return to their seats.

Handout: "Pass the Peace, Please!"

Photocopy the illustration below onto colored paper (one per child) and cut out. Children may use their handouts as bookmarks or post them in a prominent place at home.

17. Share a Smile

Theme
- using the gifts God has given us to help others

Scripture
- John 13:31-35

Setting
- kitchen table or living room

Props
- table
- chairs or bench

Characters
- Mom
- Dad
- Boy
- Girl

Suggested Music
- "Smile" (Use either of the two renditions listed in the Resources section.)

Suggested Handout
- construction-paper happy face

BOY: Hey, what's the matter? Are you crying?

GIRL: (*Crying and wiping her eyes*) I am so sad.

BOY: Don't be sad.

GIRL: I can't help it. I am feeling sad because my best friend is moving away and I will miss her so much.

BOY: Oh, that is sad. You were always doing things together and you talked to her every day.

GIRL: We have so much fun; she is like a sister to me.

BOY: Gee, I guess it will be hard for both of you. Maybe you can write her letters?

GIRL: That just won't be the same. Oh, I just don't know what I'll do.

BOY: Don't you have some other friends?

GIRL: Yes, but she was my best friend!

BOY: Oh, I bet someone will move in her house soon and then you'll have a brand new friend!

GIRL: Do you think so? That would be great.

BOY: And you know that I will always be your friend. Don't forget that!

GIRL: You know, you are a good friend. You always make me smile! (*Gives* BOY *hug.*)

BOY: I like to see you smile.

MOM enters sobbing.

BOY: Hi, Mom. What's wrong? Oh no, are you sad, too?

MOM: I just got off the phone from talking with my good friend. She is very sick and will have to go in the hospital. I feel just awful.

GIRL: That's really weird.

MOM: What is so weird about that?

GIRL: Well, I was feeling very sad, too. I was crying so hard and feeling awful when my brother here gave me a special gift.

MOM: Oh, really. What was this special gift?

GIRL: He cheered me up and made me smile! And then he gave me a big hug!

MOM: Did it help?

GIRL: It made me feel so much better!

MOM: Well, do you think it would work on me?

BOY: Here, let's just try it and see.

BOY and GIRL *give* MOM *a big hug and smile. All start to laugh and giggle.*

DAD: (*Entering*) Do I hear laughing in here?

BOY: You sure do. We are giving each other the gift of smiling; it's making us real happy.

DAD: Gifts? Can I have one?

GIRL: Well, Mom and I were feeling sad until we got a big hug and smile, and now we just can't stop laughing.

MOM: I feel so much better. A smile is the best gift you can give away. It's a great way to share your love.

BOY: That reminds me of that song we sometimes sing in church. How does it go? (*He starts the song and the others join in, motioning the entire assembly to participate.*)

Handout: "Share a Smile"

Cut out happy face pattern, then use it to make construction-paper happy faces. Use felt pen to draw eyes, nose and smile, or use cut-out smile pattern to make construction-paper smiles to glue onto happy faces.

18. Share Your Joy

Theme
- We have been given many gifts; one of them is joy.
- ways to share this joy

Scripture
- Matthew 25:14-30
- Mark 4:21-25

Setting
- kitchen table

Props
- chairs
- two cakes made out of cardboard or paper
- cooking utensils
- puppet stage if using puppets

Characters
- Mom
- Dad
- Boy
- Girl

Suggested Music
- "Joy, Joy, Joy"
- "Color the World with Song"
- "Our God Is a God of Love"
- "Smile!"
- "Gifts in My Heart"
- "Joy Is My Strength—Give It Away"

Suggested Handout
- construction-paper presents decorated with real or colored-on ribbons

---

MOM is humming as she bakes a cake. BOY *and* GIRL *enter.*

BOY: I smell something good. Are you baking something? Is it cake?

MOM: (*Nods her head*) It sure is.

GIRL: You seem happy. Is today someone's birthday? Are we having a party?

MOM: No, no birthdays, no parties! I am just full of joy today!

GIRL: Joy?

BOY: What does that mean?

GIRL: Do we have joy inside us, too?

MOM: We all have within us the gift of joy!

BOY: Gift of joy? Is it a gift? How did we get this gift?

GIRL: Who gave it to us?

MOM: It is one of the many gifts that God has given us, and it's also meant to be given away!

DAD: (*Enters singing*) I've got that joy, joy, joy down in my heart. (*Smiling*) Did I hear you all talking about joy?

BOY: Yes, and we still don't quite understand just what this joy is!

DAD: Well, it's when you are happy and you share it. Like when you give someone a big hug or you tell someone you love them.

MOM: When you are joyful, you help others feel happy. I decided to bake a cake for our neighbor who is feeling lonely and share some of my joy with her. I have lots of joy to share with others and help them feel happy.

DAD: Let's sing a song about joy and then maybe you'll understand a little better.

All sing, "I've got that joy, joy, joy down in my heart."

MOM: Joy is a gift from God and we spread it around when we share it with others, when we give it away!

BOY: Give it away?

DAD: Yes, if you keep all your joy inside, no one will ever see it. You have to share it with your family and friends, even your Mom and Dad! There are many ways to give your joy away. If you see someone who is sad, give that person some of your joy—like a hug, for example. If you see someone who is grouchy or mad, they may need some extra joy, maybe a hug and a kiss!

GIRL: Mom, since you are so full of joy and you want to give it away, I hope you baked a cake for us, too! That would sure help us feel happy!

MOM: Well, you both know you are the joy of our lives, and guess what? I just happened to make two cakes.

DAD: So, why don't you share your joy with us by giving your Mom and me a big hug?

BOY and GIRL: (*Giving hugs*) So the Good News today is: "Share the joy that God gave you every day."

Handout: "Share Your Joy"

Cut out pattern, then use it to make construction-paper gifts. Tape a small bow or piece of ribbon on each handout, or draw them on. Print "Joy" in felt pen.

19. Specially Made

Theme

- God made each child special.
- We all have been given special gifts to share.
- first children's worship or liturgy in the new school year

Scripture

- Romans 12:3-8
- Galatians 5:22-23

Setting

- liturgy

Props

- puppet stage if puppets are being used

Characters

- Mom
- Dad
- Boy
- Girl

Suggested Music

- "Celebrate God"
- "I Like Me"

Suggested Handout

- construction-paper bear

DAD: (*Speaking to audience*) Hello, boys and girls! We are so excited to be here this morning and we welcome you back from your summer vacation.

MOM: We are the Good News family, and we are back again this year to share a lot of Good News with you.

GIRL: I'm so happy 'cause religion classes are beginning again. We are going to be learning more about God. We will be singing new songs, making crafts, and meeting new friends. We'll have so much fun!

BOY: Well, I am just a little scared. Do you really think we'll have fun?

GIRL: Sure we will! Don't be scared! You'll make some new friends. I heard that there are some really special teachers who will be helping us learn about God. They have a lot of fun things planned for us.

DAD: Boys and girls, this will be a great year and we will have lots of fun if you can remember to bring all your special gifts with you every time you come to class.

BOY: Special gifts? What special gifts do we have? And why do we have to bring them to class with us?

MOM: Well, first of all, you have a special gift right here (*pointing to the boy's ears*)—your ears.

BOY: My ears?

MOM: Yes. Now, children, can you all point to your ears? You will need your ears to listen to your teachers and hear music in your classes.

DAD: Another special gift you will need to bring is your eyes. (*Points to the girl's eyes.*)

GIRL: My eyes?

DAD: Yes. Can all of you point to your eyes? You will need your eyes to see all the things that your teacher will show you and to see all the new friends you will meet.

BOY: What other special gifts do we need to bring?

MOM: Your voice! So you can all sing songs that your music teacher will teach you. You will need your voice to say your prayers and talk with your friends. Can you all point to your mouth?

GIRL: I bet I can guess one more special gift we have—our hands. We need our hands to write, draw, color and clap. (*Claps her hands together.*)

DAD: That's right! Your hands are very special. Let's all point to our hands.

BOY: Oh, let me see if I can remember all of our special gifts: our ears to listen, our eyes to see—

GIRL: Let me say some, too! My voice to sing and pray and talk, and last of all, my hands to draw and write and color and clap.

MOM: Let's clap our hands all together.

DAD: Boys and girls, can you name all those special gifts along with us? When we come to class we'll bring our special gifts of (*points to ears*) our ears, (*points to*

eyes) our eyes, *(points to mouth)* our voice and
(points to hands) our hands.

BOY: I won't forget because all those gifts make *me!* I am
going to like coming to class every week. I'm not even
scared anymore. I have lots of special gifts to bring
with me.

DAD: That's right. Every one of us has many special gifts,
and God made each one of us special.

MOM: Let's all sing a song to God to celebrate our being
specially made.

*All sing "Celebrate God." Different gestures can be
incorporated into the song. The children can stand
and do the gestures and sing along.*

DAD: So, children, the Good News today is: You are special.
Remember to bring all your special gifts with you every
time you come to class.

*If time allows, teachers for each class can be intro-
duced to the children and the assembly.*

Handout: "Specially Made"

Cut out pattern, then use it to make construction-paper bears. Use felt pen to print the words and draw the face and heart.

Part Six

A Little Preparation and a Little Rejoicing: Advent and Christmas

20. Clean Up Your Act

Themes

- Advent
- being a messenger for Jesus
- preparing

Scripture

- Matthew 3:1-6
- Luke 3:2-6
- John 1:19-28

Setting

- front of the church

Props

- microphone
- costume for John the Baptist (sandals, piece of fur material to resemble camel hair, leather belt, walking stick, wig and beard)

Characters

- Announcer
- John the Baptist
- Mom
- Boy
- Girl
- Dad

Suggested Music

- "Walk with Jesus"
- "Come O Lord"
- "Come, Lord Jesus"
- "Come to My Heart"
- "Let Heaven Rejoice"

Suggested Handout

- construction-paper megaphone

After the gospel reading, leader invites children to come up and sit on the floor in the front of the worship center.

ANNOUNCER: Good morning, children! Welcome to our children's liturgy. I was chosen to be the announcer for today. If we didn't have any announcers, things would be a real mess. Imagine going to a basketball game where no one announced the plays. Wouldn't it be hard to know what was happening? If the weather reporter on TV didn't announce tomorrow's weather, we might carry our umbrellas for a day full of sunshine.

When our doorbell rings at home, it is announcing to us that there is someone at the door. Announcing and announcers are a part of our life. Speaking of announcers, while I was listening to the Good News being announced this morning, I heard about another announcer. John the Baptist was sent by God to announce that Jesus was coming.

JOHN: (From the back of the worship center in a loud voice) Repent! Reform! Reconcile! Renew! Remember! (*Repeats until reaching the front of the worship center.*)

ANNOUNCER: Excuse me, sir. Excuse me, who are you?

JOHN: (*Walks over to the announcer.*) They call me John. I came to announce to the people to get ready because the Lord is coming soon.

ANNOUNCER: Sooo, you are an announcer, too? I bet you're John the Baptist.

JOHN: Yes, I am.

ANNOUNCER: Could you wait right there just a minute please? (*Goes over to the group of children or to the puppets at the stage and whispers to them. Then he walks back over to* JOHN.) Well, while you are here could you answer a few questions for my friends?

JOHN: Oh, I would be glad to.

ANNOUNCER calls the persons or puppets by name. Holds the microphone in front of each person or puppet as she or he asks the question.

MOM: You dress a bit odd. Is that the way people in your day dressed? Wasn't it a little warm for the desert?

JOHN: Come to think of it, it is a bit warm, and itchy. (*Scratches his shoulder.*) And it's uncomfortable for someone who lives in the desert. But you know, many people wondered about the way I dressed, and that's one of the reasons they came out to see me. They were trying to figure out just what I was doing. They'd come out to see me and then I would preach to them, sometimes quite loudly, and I would tell them, "Prepare the way for the Lord is coming." (*Looks at the* BOY.) By the way, you wouldn't happen to have any grasshoppers and wild honey around here, would you? I am a little hungry.

BOY: (*Scratches his head and looks puzzled.*) Ummm, sorry, I think grasshoppers are out of season now, and I sure don't have any wild honey. How about a piece of pizza or a big burger instead?

JOHN: (*Shaking his head*) Nooo, that's okay, I only need enough food to keep me alive so that I can tell the people today that Jesus is coming. God sent me to tell you all: Repent! Reform! Reconcile! Renew! Remember!

GIRL: John, you sure use a lot of "R" words. Could you please explain to us what you mean?

JOHN: All those "R" words simply mean: Change. Change your lives.

ANNOUNCER: What we might say today would simply be: "Clean up your act."

JOHN: I guess I never thought of putting it that way, but I can clearly see that times have changed.

DAD: I bet the people got confused back then and thought they should follow you. In fact, I bet they thought you were Jesus.

JOHN: My job was to announce that someone far greater than I was coming. His name was Jesus. Jesus would walk hand in hand with them. Some of the people listened and others just walked away. Even today, there are still people who won't listen when I speak. They turn around and walk away. It makes me so sad.

ANNOUNCER: John, we thank you for coming here today and for answering our questions. You were the announcer for Jesus many years ago, and we will be the announcers for Jesus today. We will announce to everyone the Good News. It's time to clean up our acts and walk hand in hand with Jesus.

Play or sing song. ANNOUNCER *and* JOHN *listen to the song and, when the song is almost through, walk hand in hand together down center aisle to the beat of the music.* JOHN *turns and waves goodbye to all.)*

Handout: "Clean Up Your Act"

Cut out pattern, then use it to cut megaphones from white construction paper. Use felt pen to outline and print the words.

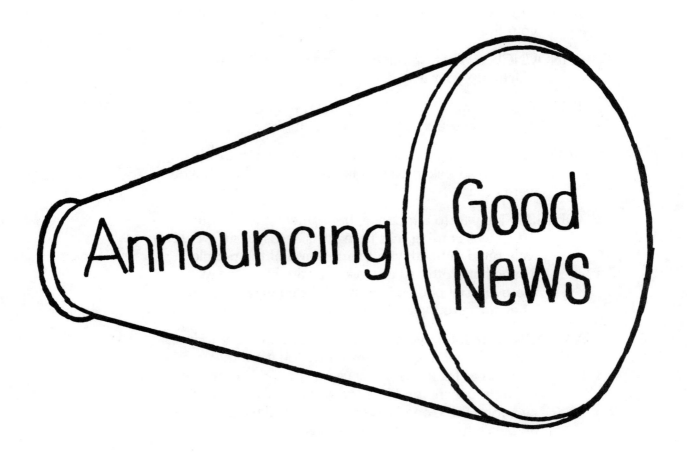

21. Gettin' Ready

Themes

- Advent
- Jesus comes to us in many ways, not just at Christmas.

Scripture

- Mark 1:2-8
- John 1:23-28

Setting

- a household expecting the arrival of a baby

Props

- window
- doll or puppet for baby
- puppet stage if puppets are used

Characters

- Grandma
- Boy
- Girl
- Mom
- Dad

Suggested Music

- "Gettin' Ready for the Miracle"
- "Jesus Is with Us Today"
- "Come, Lord Jesus"

Suggested Handout:

- paper scroll

GRANDMA is humming as BOY *enters.*

BOY: You're here just in time. Mom told us you would be here to welcome home our new baby.

GIRL: Today is the big day!

BOY: I'm just so excited; I can hardly wait till they get here. We've been so busy getting things ready for our new baby for many months now.

GRANDMA: Uh-huh!

GIRL: I've been helping Mom fold all the diapers and hang up all the baby's new clothes, and Mom even made a pretty blanket to keep the baby warm.

GRANDMA: Uh-huh!

BOY: Yeah, I've helped Dad paint the crib and set it up in the baby's room. We even hung some pictures on the walls to make the room look really special.

GRANDMA: Uh-huh!

GIRL: Grams, you will just never know how much work it takes to get ready for a baby.

GRANDMA: Oh, I think I—

BOY: (Interrupting) We've been preparing and getting ready, and you just wouldn't believe all the things we've done!

GRANDMA: Oh, I think I can try to remember. Let's see, it was a long time ago but when you have ten children you kind of remember how much work getting ready for a new baby really is.

BOY: Wow! You had to get ready ten times?

GIRL: I guess you really would get good at it.

BOY: (*Looking out the window*) Where could they be? We have been waiting forever.

GIRL: I wish they'd hurry up.

GRANDMA: It sure is hard to wait, isn't it?

BOY: It sure is! Hey, how about a story, Grams?

GRANDMA: Well, listening to the two of you makes me think of this time of year, right before Christmas. It's called Advent, when everyone is getting ready and waiting to celebrate Jesus' birthday.

BOY: Oh, we learned about that. Advent is when someone special is coming, and it's baby Jesus, right?

GRANDMA: That's right. And it's even more than that. Advent is also a time to remind us that Jesus comes to us every day.

GIRL: Every day? I didn't know he comes to us every day!

GRANDMA: Yes. Jesus comes to us in many ways: whenever we help someone, or whenever someone is kind to us, when we say our prayers, and when we go to church. He comes even when we see a pretty flower or gaze up at the stars at night. And he comes to us at communion time—if we're old enough to receive communion.

BOY: So then Advent is a time to look at all the ways Jesus comes to us.

GIRL: Not just at Christmas?

GRANDMA: Not only then but *every* day! You kids have been busy preparing and getting ready to celebrate your new baby coming home to be a part of your family. Jesus is just like your new baby. Every time we share our love or we notice all the beauty around us, we bring Jesus into our home.

BOY: (*Looking out the window*) Oh, they're here! It's Mom and Dad and our new baby!

GIRL: And are we ever ready!

MOM and DAD: (*Enter the house carrying the new baby.*) We're home!

BOY: Mom! Dad! Wow! That's our new baby?

GIRL: Oh, the baby is so tiny!

GRANDMA: What a beautiful grandbaby!

BOY: (*Looks at the baby.*) Welcome to your new family. I'm your big brother.

GIRL: (*Looks at the baby.*) Grams, looking at our new baby I think I understand just what you mean now! We worked very hard to get ready for our new baby. During Advent we need to work very hard to prepare our hearts for Jesus' coming. And we gotta remember that Jesus comes to us in many ways!

ALL: Children, are you getting ready?

At this time, the children in the choir sing "Gettin' Ready for the Miracle" or some other appropriate music.

Handout: "Gettin' Ready"

Photocopy onto white paper, cut out and roll into scrolls. If this script is used in Advent, tie scrolls with purple ribbon; if used near Christmas, tie with gold ribbon.

Get ready to see Jesus today!

22. A Little Quiet Whisper

Theme
- Christmas

Scripture
- Isaiah 9:5

Setting
- manger scene

Props
- manger
- crib
- hay
- animal figures (optional)
- battery-operated candles for the angels to carry, or stars on wands made out of tin foil and cardboard
- doll for baby Jesus
- microphone placed near the crib

Characters
- Mary
- Joseph
- three shepherds
- five angels
- Boy
- Girl

Suggested Music
- "Gettin' Ready for the Miracle"
- "Children, Run Joyfully"
- "Violet in the Snow"

Suggested Handout
- construction-paper star ornament

Presentation

This skit is used to begin the liturgy. The first suggested song, "Gettin' Ready for the Miracle," makes an excellent gathering hymn. Others may be used if they reflect the spirit of the season and the quietness of the "little whispers" theme.

The procession includes MARY and JOSEPH carrying baby Jesus, followed by the ANGELS and SHEPHERDS, and then the "modern-day" BOY and GIRL. They all proceed to the manger, where MARY and JOSEPH place the baby in the crib. MARY and JOSEPH kneel down on either side of the crib. The angels stand around the back of the crib in a semi-circle. The SHEPHERDS kneel down to one side of the crib. The BOY and GIRL go directly behind the crib and look down at the baby Jesus.

MARY and JOSEPH look at each other, and then MARY places her hand over her mouth to whisper to JOSEPH. Into the microphone she says in a loud whisper, "His name is Jesus!" JOSEPH then turns to the SHEPHERDS and whispers, "His name is Jesus!" They turn to the ANGELS and whisper, "His name is Jesus!" This continues on until all the characters, including the BOY and GIRL have whispered to each other, "His name is Jesus!"

Then the choir begins the Gloria and all the characters join in the singing.

Homily Idea

The priest or homilist can discuss or dialogue at the regular homily time about what happened in the skit. This discussion should include an understanding of the symbolism of including "today's" children in the nativity scene, or perhaps it could focus on the name of Jesus, highlighting first "What's in a name?" and then "What's in Jesus' name?" Use some of the titles contained in the antiphons or Isaiah 9:5.

Handout: "A Quiet Little Whisper"

Cut out pattern, then use it to make construction-paper stars. Print the words on each star, punch a hole in the top, and thread with ribbon or yarn.

23. Just a Little More

Themes

- Christmas
- We all get caught up in wanting more.

Setting

- Christmas or Advent liturgy

Props

- If you use the adaptation, you will need costumes for two or three morzy bugs. They should wear all black slacks and shirts. Perhaps they could wear black knit hats that cover the face, with only the eyes and nose showing. This effect can also be achieved with black face make-up. Each should have a cone-shaped nose made out of black construction paper and attached by a black piece of elastic, secured on each side with a staple. Finally, the costume could include a black headband with black pipe cleaners wrapped around it, leaving a long end sticking straight up for antennae or feelers with silver bells attached on the ends.

Characters

- Priest or homilist

If you use the adaptation:

- two or three Morzy bugs

Suggested Music

- If you use the adaptation, use background music (*instrumental*) on guitar or piano as the morzy bugs enter and leave.

Suggested Handout

- The minister, priest or homilist should ask the children to get a piece of paper when they go home and write down something they can give Jesus for his birthday. They should place the paper near the manger under the Christmas tree.

Introduction

The following Homily Idea is adapted from a book by Julie Kelemen called *Advent Is for Children: Stories, Activities, Prayers.*

The definition of a morzy bug is any imaginary bug that attacks humans. This insect's bite causes a person to want more of many things, even if the person already has plenty. Morzy bites have also been known to keep people from sharing with one another.

Homily Idea: "Something to Do—A Morzy Quiz"

The sermon or homily could begin with the homilist introducing the morzy quiz.

HOMILIST: Here's a quiz to help you figure out if you've ever been bitten by morzies. Answer yes or no to each question.

1. Does your hand ache after you've written down all the items on your Christmas wish list?

2. Are you more interested in what's inside a package than who gave it to you?

3. Have you ever been mad because you didn't get exactly what you wanted for Christmas?

4. On the day after Christmas do you find yourself already thinking of what you want next year?

5. Are you sad if you get "just clothes" as a Christmas present?

6. Have you ever felt jealous that someone else got more or nicer gifts than you did?

7. Have you ever found yourself not wanting to let a friend play with your presents?

8. Have you ever been angry with someone who bought you a cheap gift when you knew the person could afford something better?

9. Do you forget to thank people for the gifts you receive?

10. On the day after Christmas have you ever gotten a sad feeling that makes you want to say, "Is that all there is to Christmas?"

If you answered "yes" to five or more of these questions, you have a bad case of the morzies. If you said "yes" three to five times, you're about average. If you answered "yes" to two or less, you're probably not telling the truth. The truth is, everyone has been bitten by a morzy. Even parents, priests, the principal, and your teacher have been bitten by a morzy at one time or another. Fortunately, there is more to Advent and

Christmas than receiving expensive gifts. If you already know that, you're on the right track to understanding what Christmas and Christ's message are all about.

At the end of the homily, the speaker then asks the children to get some paper when they go home and write down something that they could give Jesus for Christmas, such as love, prayer, or thanks, so that they can focus on giving rather than getting.

Adaptation

The deacon, associate pastor, religious education director or youth minister presents this homily for the children. As the speaker begins to describe the morzy bug, the characters might come from the back of the worship center, stopping along the way and gently touching the children and adults with the end of their long noses. They say the word "morzies" again and again, emphasizing the "zzz" to sound like bugs. Then they wander out of the worship center before the morzy quiz begins, to allow the speaker to be heard.

As in the Homily Idea, at the end of the sermon, the speaker then asks the children to get some paper when they go home and write down something that they could give Jesus for Christmas, such as love, prayer, or thanks, so that they can focus on giving rather than getting.

This adaptation can be done without the morzy bugs, but children generally respond to "live" bugs and get more meaning from the presentation if the bugs participate.

Part Seven

A Little Repenting and a Little Alleluia: Lent and Easter

24. Seeing Jesus

Themes

- Lent
- ways in which we see Jesus in others
- ways in which we experience God's love

Scripture

- Mark 8:22-26

Setting

- around a table in kitchen or living room

Props

- puppet stage if puppets are used

Characters

- Grandpa
- Grandma
- Boy
- Girl

Suggested Music

- "Jesus Is with Us"
- "Jesus, Jesus"
- "Amazing Grace"

Suggested Handouts

- blindfolds made from scrap material, with these words written on a piece of paper and attached with a safety pin: "Don't be blind. Open your eyes and see Jesus."
- construction-paper faces

BOY: (*Enters and gives grandparents a big hug.*) Hi! It's good to see you.

GIRL: (*Enters and gives hugs, too.*) We are sooo glad to see you!

BOY: We've missed you! We always have the best time when we come to visit you. And you always have the best stories to tell us.

GIRL: We've waited so long to see you, Grandma. Can you tell us a story right now?

BOY: Yeah, how about a story? (*Begging*) Please?

GRANDPA: Well, we are happy to see you two rascals! How about it, Grandma? Do you have a story for the kids?

GRANDMA: (*Thinking*) Hmmm.

GRANDPA: Why don't you tell them about the time you were just a little girl, just about their size? Remember? You were so sick and you had a very high fever.

GRANDMA: Oh, that would be a good one. Yes, that's the time when I first saw Jesus.

BOY: You saw Jesus? Where?

GIRL: Wow, what did he look like? Did he have a beard?

GRANDMA: Hold on now. Let me tell the story, and then you will see. (*Pulls the children close to her, then begins.*) You see, my mommy and daddy had told me stories about Jesus ever since I was just a baby. I knew a lot about him. I hadn't ever seen him, but one time I was very sick and I did see him. I was in bed for many days. In those days we had to stay in bed until our fever was all gone.

GRANDPA: We didn't have all the medicine and doctors like you children have today.

GRANDMA: Someone in my family stayed with me the whole time I was sick. She never left my side. I would feel her wiping my forehead with a cool cloth. She gave me lots of liquids and some awful-tasting medicine. (*Wrinkles her face to show how bad it tasted.*) Even when I would wake up in the middle of the night, someone was always there to give me a sip of cold water.

BOY: Tell us, Grandma, was it Jesus? Was it? Did you get a close look at him?

GRANDMA: Yes, I did indeed see Jesus! I saw Jesus in my mother's love and caring. You see, children, the "someone" was my mother. She had stayed by my side, day and night, until I was well again.

GRANDPA: There are many ways we can see Jesus. Do you know that Grandma and I see Jesus whenever we look into your eyes? We also see Jesus in a rainbow or in a beautiful sunset.

GIRL: I don't get it. I've seen pictures of Jesus in books. Did you actually see his face?

GRANDMA: Honey, it takes faith to see Jesus. If you know Jesus, then you can see him in others. You can see him all around you, even in nature, too.

GRANDPA: Children, maybe if I say it this way, you can understand. Where is air?

BOY: Oh, that's easy. It's all around us!

GRANDPA: Tell me now. How do you know that? Can you see it?

GIRL: No, but we all know it's there.

GRANDPA: Now you've got it! You know and have faith that it's there. We just know that Jesus is here with us. He told us that he would always be with us.

GRANDMA: If we know Jesus, then we can see Jesus. If we look with eyes of faith, we will see him!

GIRL: Wow! That was a great story. I see now what you mean.

BOY: Me, too, and I have a funny feeling that Jesus is with us right this very minute!

BOY and GIRL: *(Look at each other and shake their heads in agreement.)* Grandpa, Grandma, we see Jesus in you! *(They give hugs to their grandparents.)*

To reinforce the message, sing "Jesus Is with Us."

Handout: "Seeing Jesus"

Cut out the circle shape, then use it as a pattern for construction-paper faces. On one side of each face, draw the eyes open; on the other side, draw the eyes closed.

25. What's Your Excuse?

Themes

- Lent
- Jesus is always inviting us to come follow him.

Scripture

- Luke 14:15-24
- John 8:12-20

Setting

- liturgy

Props

- puppet stage if puppets are used

Characters

- Mom
- Dad
- Boy
- Girl

Suggested Music

- "Follow Me"
- "The Wedding Banquet"
- "Beginning Today"
- "Come Along with Me to Jesus"

Suggested Handout

- Give invitations to the children the week before liturgy. One invitation can be placed on a bulletin board or in the bulletin for the larger community.

DAD: (*Speaking to audience*) Good morning, children! We are sure glad to be here today.

BOY: We always have a lot of Good News to share with children.

MOM: The Good News today is: Jesus is always inviting us to come follow him.

DAD: Speaking of being invited, we know that all of you were invited to come to this celebration today. Well, when we received our invitation, we had a few problems.

BOY: Yeah, my sister had a real good excuse why she couldn't come today.

GIRL: Well, you had a few excuses yourself!

BOY: She was afraid, and she gets real shy. Sometimes her face turns all red.

GIRL: (*Acts shy and blushes.*) Oh? At least I was excited about coming here. What was your excuse?

BOY: I just figured I'd be too busy.

GIRL: Busy? Busy doing what? That's a silly reason. That sounds like just a flimsy excuse to me.

BOY: And so is yours.

GIRL: No, it is not.

BOY: Is too.

GIRL: Is not.

MOM: Children, settle down! Let's talk about this. We heard in the Good News today that there was a very important man who was having a party. Many of the invited guests had good excuses and good reasons why they couldn't come to the celebration.

DAD: Jesus used this story to show the people that he is always inviting us to come follow him, and sometimes we are too busy or too afraid to come follow him. We come up with many excuses why we can't accept his invitation.

BOY: I don't understand? How do we follow Jesus?

MOM: Well, every Sunday you are invited to come share with all your family and friends in the celebration of Eucharist at liturgy. He invites us to learn more about him in our religion classes.

DAD: We follow Jesus every time we tell our friends about Jesus' love and when we share our love with our family and friends. We follow Jesus when we celebrate joyfully at Sunday liturgy.

MOM: By doing these things we say "Yes" to Jesus' invitation to follow him.

GIRL: Oh, I get it! And when I say "Yes" to Jesus, I'm not so afraid after all. I'm glad I came here today!

BOY: No more flimsy excuses for me either. I'm sure happy to be here and to celebrate with Jesus and all of the children!

MOM: We have a song to sing for you and you can join in and sing along with us.

Handout: "What's Your Excuse?"

Cut out rectangle pattern, then use it to make construction-paper invitations. Fold in half as shown. On the front, print the words and add balloons or other design. On the inside print the words and include your parish name and date and time of liturgy.

26. Empty Surprises

Themes

- Easter Sunday
- the empty tomb and its meaning

Scripture

- Matthew 28:1-10
- John 20:1-10

Setting

- liturgy

Characters

- Homilist

Props

- cookie jar
- empty milk carton
- empty ice-cream cone
- piggy bank

Suggested Music

- "God Is a Surprise"
- "Jesus Christ Is Risen Today"
- "Signs of New Life"
- "Brand New Song"
- "Oh, Yes, Lord Jesus Lives"

Suggested Handout

- empty plastic egg or (after liturgy) hollow chocolate egg

Presentation/Homily Idea

A suggested approach to the "quieter" themes of Easter is to have the homilist talk gently about how disappointing it is to go to get a cookie from the cookie jar and find the jar empty. The homilist explores this with the children and offers one or two an empty cookie jar. He or she next asks if anyone has ever been really thirsty for a drink of cold milk only to find the milk carton empty, or needed money to buy something and found the piggy bank empty. Again, it is important to include opportunities for the children to visualize the emptiness. Still another example is to ask if anyone has ever had a double-dip ice cream cone and spilled all the ice cream out. After turning the cone upside down, the homilist suggests that not all surprises are so empty.

The homilist then retells the Good News of the visit to the empty tomb. The women who peeked inside the tomb were looking for Jesus, and they found only cold rock walls. They were afraid, confused and disappointed because Jesus' body was gone. However, the tomb was empty because Jesus had risen from the dead. Jesus proved that he was God's son, and he conquered death. It was really the empty tomb that was the Good

News of this story. Jesus was alive again and ready to help us in our everyday struggles.

The homilist encourages everyone to think about the great "empty" surprise of Easter.

27. Sunshine and Her Seven Friends

Themes

- death and resurrection
- We grieve for a while but then we move on to do the work that Jesus has sent us here to do.

Scripture

- John 5:24

Setting

- on a bench outside

Props

- basket of apples
- piece of silk or glittery material in gold or white
- some silk flowers

Characters

- Sunshine (costume: dress and apron)
- Green-Eyed Gretta, the queen (costume: tattered dress)
- Jesus (costume: white jeans and shirt)
- Narrator

Sunshine's friends, listed below, are casually dressed and wear around their necks signs with their names printed in large letters.

- Jittery
- Dozy
- Goofy
- Sniffy
- Grouchy
- Cheery
- Smarty

Suggested Handout

- construction-paper tool box with tools

This story clearly parallels the fairy tale about Snow White and the seven dwarfs. This similarity is intentional, as the idea here is to allow the children to be really comfortable with the story. Some of the fear and anxiety about death can be overcome for young people if they recognize "the plot."*

Scene i

SUNSHINE: (*Sitting on a bench with the seven friends around her; some may sit on the floor or beside her.*) I just want to thank you all for letting me stay

---

* While this presentation does not directly address the season of Lent or Easter, it does address our Christian beliefs about death and resurrection based on the paschal mystery.

here with you and for keeping me safe from the queen. You have been such good friends to me.

JITTERY: (*Nervous and shy*) Why doesn't the queen like you?

SUNSHINE: The queen is jealous of me; she thinks I am the most beautiful one in the village.

DOZY: (*Tired and groggy*) You are very beautiful, Sunshine, and your hair is so-o-o pretty.

SUNSHINE: Oh, I know that I am beautiful, but it's not my hair or the way I look that makes me beautiful! My beauty is on the inside. You see, I have a heart that's full of love. When the queen looks in the mirror, she sees that she is not a very loving person. She has made a lot of wrong choices in her life. She has chosen to be mean and angry to everyone she meets, instead of having a heart full of love.

The seven friends leave for work, humming their song.

Scene ii

GREEN-EYED GRETTA: Apples for sale! Delicious apples for sale. (*Knocks at the door.*) Try a bite of my juicy apples; they are great for snacks or desserts.

SUNSHINE: Oh, those sure look good. (*Takes a big bite of one and then falls to the floor.*)

GREEN-EYED GRETTA: Juicy apple all right! Now we will see who is the most beautiful woman in the village. Ha ha!

NARRATOR: The queen left as fast as she could. Soon the seven friends came back, calling Sunshine. They found her lying on the ground.

CHEERY: Oh, no! Something has happened to Sunshine!

ALL: (*Gathering around her*) Oh, she's dead! What will we do without Sunshine? This is so sad! We will never ever see her again.

They kneel down and begin to cry. They all get up and walk over to an area where she is somewhat behind them and they cannot see her. They sit out on the bench and talk all night.

SMARTY: What will we do without her? This is just so sad. (*Thinks for a minute.*) Wait a minute! Do you remember what she told us? She talked about one day going to heaven to be with Jesus. She is not here, but she is still alive. She's gone to the kingdom of love.

JESUS enters behind the seven friends, carrying a few flowers and a silk wrap. He goes over to SUNSHINE *and places the flowers in her hair, smiling at her. She gets up and she smiles as he places the silk wrap on her shoulders. This symbol helps to show the transformation that happens when we die.* JESUS *and* SUNSHINE *smile as he leads her off, behind the seven friends so they see nothing of what has just happened.*

SMARTY: She's gone to live in the kingdom of love. She will be with Jesus forever and ever. I'm happy for her 'cause she will be with Jesus. But, I'm sad for us. We will miss her so much.

CHEERY: Maybe some day we will see her again. When we die, we will be part of the kingdom of love, too.

GOOFY: Remember what she told us, that when her mom died she was sad for a while. We will be sad for a while, too. But, someday we will all be together again.

JITTERY: We will think about her and miss her beautiful heart full of love.

DOZY: Well, then maybe we can get back to the work that needs to be done. We have to share with others what Sunshine shared with us.

SNIFFY: Yes (sniffs), we have to choose to love one another so one day we will be with her again in the kingdom with Jesus.

GRUMPY: Well, guys, it's almost morning; the sun will be up soon. You know what work needs to be done. You all know what we have to do, so let's get to work.

ALL: Heigh Ho, heigh ho, it's off to work we go. Heigh ho, heigh ho, it's off to work we go.

They sing for as long as it takes to exit down center aisle.

Handout: "Sunshine and Her Seven Friends"

Photocopy onto white paper (one per child) and give to children to color.

Unwrapping Little Gifts © 1994
Resource Publications, Inc. All rights reserved.

Part Eight

Un Piloncito: A Little Gift of Hispanic Culture

Unwrapping the Gift of Culture

Traditions, rituals, and cultural celebrations are passed down from generation to generation through the sharing of stories. The title of this section, *"Un Piloncito,"* means "a little gift or grace." A dear friend shared one of her stories with us that highlights the "little gifts" theme. As a child, when she went to the market with her parents, she would always receive a little extra gift, or a "freebie" as some today would call it. This little tradition is still very much alive in her family and it is this richness of culture and tradition we attempt to capture in this chapter. Because much of the Latino culture has been integrated into everyday life throughout the United States—from fabulous foods to fun-filled fiestas—we feel it is important to include some of the more common liturgical celebrations from this rich heritage. But, first, a few thoughts about diversity and culture in general.

From our own childlike perspective—our "little" we shall call it—we visualize the people our God has created as so many flavors of ice cream. The diversity of peoples, and of individuals within the same race, is like heaven's own Baskin Robbins: thirty-one people flavors. Each flavor comes with its own special ingredients, just as each person comes with specific and individual cultural backgrounds, which make us who we are. Some of us, blended as we are from many different backgrounds, could probably be labeled Rocky Road or Rainbow Sherbet, in the Baskin Robbins analogy. Fortunately, there is a place for all the flavors—from plain old vanilla to Swiss mocha cream—in God's ice cream shoppe! Each particular ethnic group brings a treasure of cultures and customs to the human experience. Children are eager to learn about and accept the cultural differences and similarities of all people. When children are shown how to respect each other as children of God, peace and harmony are created. Unless children are taught prejudice, they cannot be prejudiced.

The diversity of cultures in our country offers the opportunity for so many gifts to be unwrapped and shared, so many stories to be told, so much to be learned from each other. Liturgical celebration should encourage the telling of those stories so that all our faith communities have a mixture of rich cultures, cultures which are a vital part of the daily lives of all. Polish, German, African, Chinese, Native American, Vietnamese, Latino and Irish groups enrich our churches and love to share their traditions. Perhaps the list of cultures at your church is even longer. If your community has such a variety of cultures, the depth and richness of that heritage could be celebrated with an international fair. Each group could share its native foods, costumes, rituals and stories with the larger community, and thus each unique cultural background can be celebrated. The overall theme will highlight the connectedness and sense of belonging all of God's family share.

Those blessed with a variety of ancestral backgrounds—a quarter of one culture or a third of another—could expand on this cultural fair concept and experience new ways to create these ethnic traditions within their own families. The exchanging of such customs and rituals benefits everyone. When we rob people of their heritage by insisting that only one cultural worship setting is appropriate, we negate the very rainbow of people with which our Creator God has inhabited the earth. The many traditions, rituals and customs represented by all the people of our faith communities are rich sources of, and testimony to, a living faith.

Our own personal "roots" include growing up in a small town in Kansas. We were always excited to meet people who had moved in from "far-away" places. Many different "rainbow" people enriched our lives, and we learned a lot from each of them. One particular friend, Gloria, from the Latino culture, was special. Gloria had the most beautiful hair and eyes, and she was gifted with such a sense of humor and laughter. When we visited Gloria's grandmother—Mammer was her name, and she spoke no English—we were drawn to her kitchen by a fragrant aroma of spices and foods we had never experienced before. There on a flat cast-iron skillet, Mammer would make us a white, round piece of thin bread. With puzzled looks on our faces, we watched as she broke the bread and shared it with us. We learned in that tiny kitchen that language is not a barrier when bread is shared as a gift of love.

Moving to San Antonio, Texas, we were reintroduced to the rich and festive heritage of the Latino culture within our own church community and city. This vibrant heritage has provided us new and exciting experiences of the way in which Latinos celebrate the fullness of life. The beautiful and unique way this culture expresses faith in religious and family settings is powerful. With vivid color and joyful music, this celebrating spills over from the place of worship into the surrounding homes and communities. These festive occasions almost always reflect the celebration of life itself.

In this section, a few of the many liturgical celebrations that enrich Latino culture are unwrapped. For some, it is a new gift. For others, it is a time-tested treasure from the past. These celebrations are included because the Latino heritage is one of the largest, most accessible resources from which we can draw. Again, your flexibility and ability to adapt what follows to "fit" your faith community is essential.

One exciting by-product of introducing ethnic celebrations into your church community is that you rarely need to search for volunteers. Most people are honored to share their heritage. When we enable these people to unwrap their gifts, the entire church is blessed and enriched.

28. Our Lady of Guadalupe

This feast day is celebrated on December 12 each year. It is an annual event that is of great importance to the people of Mexico. It is also a special day throughout the United States, the Latin Americas and Canada.

A well-planned Guadalupe celebration is worth the time, effort and money spent. This rich and beautiful tribute to Our Lady and the fellowship that generally accompanies the celebration give a cultural perspective to the feast which crosses all ethnic barriers.

Themes

- giving birth to a new beginning for those oppressed
- liberation, freedom

Scripture

- First reading: Revelation 11:19, 12:1-6,10
- Responsorial Psalm: Luke 1 (*Mary's Song of Praise*)
- Gospel: Luke 1:39-56

Setting

- on a hillside, then in a rectory office

Props

- serape placed over the altar cloth
- large papier-maché hill
- large rocks
- some bushes or cactus plants
- a few chairs and a desk (*to resemble a rectory office*)
- portrait or statue of Our Lady of Guadalupe
- rose (one per "peasant" child)
- vase

Characters

- Juan Diego. Costume: large sombrero, white shirt and pants, *tilma* (cloak) worn like a cape over the shoulder, laminated poster or image of Our Lady of Guadalupe pinned onto tilma
- Mary. Costume: light brown shift imprinted with red roses, brown waistband (maternity band signifies that "someone" is yet to come). For Mary's mantle, use a turquoise cape with gold stars, which depicts the great god Omecihuatl who was the supreme god and source of all unity in the Aztec culture. Stars signify a new beginning or era.
- Bishop. Costume: hat and staff, long white robe
- Brother. Costume: long brown monk-type robe with hood
- Peasants (ten to twenty boys and girls). Boys' costumes: white shirts and pants with serape vests. Girls' costumes: white peasant blouses with bright-colored full skirts and sashes, ribbons and paper flowers in their hair, or mantillas (small cloaks) worn on the head or over the shoulder. Each child carries a rose to place in a large vase in front of the shrine during the procession.
- Narrator

Suggested Music

- "Rosa del Tepeyac"
- Other beautiful songs are available for use in this celebration. Mariachis or a bilingual choir with trumpet players and guitars enrich this liturgy. Children can be included, too.

Suggested Handouts

- holy cards of our Lady of Guadalupe
- small tissue paper flowers made in bright colors

Preparation

- Place a large portrait of Our Lady of Guadalupe to one side of the altar.

Lights may be strung around the edges, material draped from the picture, and a large vase placed directly in front of the picture. A statue, if one is available, could also be used. To add a festive flair, decorate with brightly-colored tissue paper flowers around the sides of the shrine. Only the roses should be placed in front of the shrine. Using spotlights can enhance the shrine, while other lighting effects can be used to highlight the appearance of Our Lady to Juan Diego as he travels back and forth in the story.

- Sound effects, such as the knocking at the door at the bishop's home, can be used as needed.

The liturgy begins with a festive entrance song as the children and actors process down the aisle and take their places in reserved front rows. After the Liturgy of the Word, the story is acted out in the front of the worship space. The props need to be in place before liturgy begins. *

NARRATOR *announces "The Story of Our Lady of Guadalupe," then proceeds to tell the following story as the characters act it out.*

NARRATOR: On December 12, 1531, Our Lady appeared to Juan Diego on a hilltop known as Tepeyac, just outside Mexico City. Juan Diego was on his way to Mass early one morning when he heard beautiful music. Suddenly he heard a voice bidding him, "Juanito, Juan Dieguito." Our Lady appeared to Juan and told him that she would like a temple to be built upon this hill in honor of her. She wanted Juan to go into Mexico City and tell the bishop of her request. She also told Juan that she was "Holy Mary, Ever-Virgin, Mother of the True God."

---

* The story is summarized and adapted from the text of *The Story of Our Lady of Guadalupe*, available in both English and Spanish.

Unwrapping Little Gifts © 1994

Juan promptly went to see Bishop Zumarrage to tell him about the appearance of Our Lady. The bishop kindly listened but was not convinced of Juan's story. Juan was dismissed and asked to return in a few days, thus allowing the bishop to review the event. So Juan made his way back to the Tepeyac hilltop and found Our Lady waiting there for him. He told Our Lady that the bishop was just not able to accept her request. Our Lady asked Juan to go back one more time to present her plea. The next day Juan attempted to call on the bishop, and once again he was turned away. The bishop asked for some type of sign to prove that Our Lady had actually appeared. Frustrated, Juan went back to the hilltop and spoke with Our Lady. He was all but ready to quit and explained to Our Lady that the bishop needed some kind of visual sign to believe in her appearance. Our Lady promised Juan that she would have a sign for the bishop when Juan returned the next day. But the following morning Juan couldn't leave his sick, dying uncle. He stayed by his side the entire day. That evening his uncle asked Juan to get a priest so that he could receive confession and the last sacraments.

Early the next morning, on the twelfth day of December, Juan left to find a priest for his uncle. He took a different route this time, to avoid another encounter with Our Lady. He was embarrassed and afraid because he had not returned to Tepeyac as Our Lady has asked him. Along the way, our Lady approached him and asked him where he was going. Juan explained that he was caring for his uncle who was very ill. Our Lady reassured Juan that his uncle would not die. Juan was relieved to hear this and offered to go back to the bishop to plead her request. She asked Juan to go up to the hilltop. Upon arriving, Juan was amazed to find beautiful roses in full bloom, there on the icy and bare ground. He gathered up the roses and brought them to Our Lady. She carefully placed them in his tilma, telling him that this was her promised sign. She instructed him to deliver the roses to the bishop. Juan went quickly to the bishop and opened the cloak. The roses fell to the floor. The bishop was not only overwhelmed by the miracle of the roses but fell to his knees at the sight of the tilma. Imprinted there was the beautiful image of Our Lady just as Juan had seen her on the hilltop. A shrine was built on the hilltop just in time for Christmas, on the exact spot that Our Lady had appeared.

Immediately after the story is told, the props are removed and the spotlight focuses on the shrine. At this time the children leave their seats and walk down the side aisle to the back of the church. They begin the procession down the center aisle with a simple dance. Each girl takes hold of her skirt with one hand; in her other hand she holds a rose. Each boy also carries a rose. They dance gracefully to and fro accompanied by lively music until they reach the shrine. The first boy and girl go up and place their roses in the vase. This is repeated until all the children have finished. Three or more children, who follow close behind the procession, carry the bread and wine to the altar.

After the Liturgy of the Eucharist and the closing prayer and blessing, the children process out, dancing to a joyful song.

Post-Liturgy Celebration

After the liturgy, a feast of authentic Mexican foods is an excellent way to extend the cultural immersion. The meal can be pot-luck, where everyone brings different dishes of rice, beans, chili and tamales. Or the church could pay to have certain authentic foods brought in. The band can entertain at the celebration, and a piñata filled with candies can be broken open by the children. Sharing the candy would further reinforce Christian themes.

29. Pan Bendito (Blessed Bread)

This custom is celebrated on Holy Thursday or on any Sunday during Lent.

Themes

- Bread symbolizes our service to others.
- All of us are God's children, a faith community and family.
- God loves and cares for us.

Props

- baskets for the bread

Characters

- Children to carry up big baskets of the bread and stand at the altar while it is blessed

Suggested Music

- "Danos Senor de Esos Panes"
- "Un Espiga"

Preparation

- This bread recalls the way in which God provides for us, not only in the daily bread of the Eucharist but also in all our daily needs as well. The bread can be purchased or each family can bring their own. As the scope of this book is focused on children's celebrations, we suggest that the children bake the bread at home as a family lenten project. Another option would be to bake the bread during the children's religious education classes.

Recipe for Baking Bread

Adapted from Better Homes and Gardens Mexican Cook Book.

Ingredients

- 7¼ cups all-purpose flour
- 2 packages active dry yeast
- 2½ cups water
- 1 Tablespoon sugar
- 1 Tablespoon salt
- 1 Tablespoon shortening
- yellow cornmeal
- 1 egg white
- 1 Tablespoon water

In large bowl, combine 3 cups flour with yeast. Heat water, sugar, salt, and shortening just until warm (115 to 120 degrees), stirring constantly to almost melt shortening. Add to the dry ingredients. Beat at low speed with electric mixer for 30 seconds, scraping bowl often. Beat 3 minutes at high speed. By hand, stir in enough of remaining flour to make a soft dough. Knead on floured surface 10 to 12 minutes or until smooth. Shape into ball. Place in greased bowl; turn once to grease top. Cover; let rise 1 to 1½ hours or until doubled in size. Punch down; divide dough into 18 pieces. Cover; let rest 10 minutes. Shape each piece into ovals five inches long. Pull and twist each end slightly. Place on greased and cornmeal-sprinkled baking sheets. Make lengthwise cut (¼" deep) on top of each. Beat egg white and 1 Tablespoon water until foamy; brush tops and sides of each piece. Cover; let rise about 1 hour or until double. Bake at 375 degrees for 20 minutes. Remove from oven and brush again with egg white mixture. Bake 10 to 15 minutes longer or until golden brown. Makes 18 rolls.

Presentation and Homily Idea

If this custom is celebrated on Holy Thursday, the children can be a part of the liturgy. If it is done at a children's liturgy, we recommend that the presider or homilist share this tradition with the children at the homily. Giving a brief history of the pan bendito, the homilist emphasizes that the bread is not the Eucharist, but blessed bread. The homilist instructs the children that when they leave, they should take the bread to share with others.

For the presentation of the gifts, several children carry up the bread in large baskets and stand before or around the altar, while the priest blesses the bread. The blessed bread can then be left at the foot of the altar until after the liturgy.

Usually, at the end of liturgy, the pan bendito or blessed bread is given to the people to take home to share with those who may be sick or unable to come to the liturgy. Names of sick parishioners or others not attending the liturgy are gathered, so that the bread may be delivered to them. If taking bread to the sick is not feasible, families simply share their blessed bread at home.

Note: Veladoras (candles) can also be blessed on Holy Thursday, but we suggest setting aside another Sunday during the lenten season to have these candles blessed in a similar way as the bread. Lighted veladoras are a reminder that Christ is present in the home. They are used when storms cause power outages or danger. At a children's liturgy, candles can be brought from home, tied up in a ribbon (with the child's name on the candle), and placed in baskets. The candles can be blessed during the homily along with a brief explanation of this custom, or this can take place at the end of the liturgy.

30. Los Posadas

This celebration is a re-enactment of Joseph's and Mary's search for a place where Mary could give birth to Jesus. It is celebrated in many ways. It can be done in the community in one evening or acted out over a period of nine days, ending at the Christmas midnight liturgy. The nine days represent a nine-day traditional Christmas novena.

Themes

- The journey of Mary and Joseph represents the cry of those who are cast out by society, such as the homeless.
- We recognize all people as God's children.
- The welcoming of Mary and Joseph into the home serves as a reminder for us to open our hearts to those in need.
- The pilgrimage of the Holy Family reminds us that even when we are discouraged, we must struggle on and endure the hardships of life.
- We press on along the path that leads us to new life.

Scripture

- Luke 2:1-7

Setting

- This journey can take place outside around the church grounds. The characters could stop to ask for lodging at various buildings such as the rectory, religious education building, or administration office. If no buildings are available, set up makeshift doorways outside the church. The final stop is at the doors of the church. If the weather is inclement, set up the makeshift doorways in the middle aisle of the church, leading up to the manger setting.

Props

- long-burning candles for the children who walk with Mary and Joseph to carry

Characters

- Joseph
- Mary
- children to accompany Mary and Joseph
- Townspeople (a few adults and/or children)
- Narrator

Suggested Music

- songs from *Cantos para Pedir Posadas y Otras Canciones de Navidad*
- traditional songs such as "Silent Night," "Away in a Manger," "What Child Is This," "Oh Little Town of Bethlehem" (sung in Spanish or English or both)
- "Romper la Piñata" (for celebration afterward)

Suggested Handouts

- holy card pictures of the nativity
- a candle cut-out reminding the children that they must light the way
- candy and other refreshments from the piñata celebration

The celebration begins with all gathered outside the church. The NARRATOR *(presider, deacon, or other minister) reads the gospel, which is taken from Luke 2:1-7. The journey begins to the first house, while a Christmas carol is sung. The procession stops at the first house.*

Knocking at the door, JOSEPH *sings the following song:*

En nombre del cielo	In the name of heaven
os pido posada	we beg you for lodging.
pues no puede andar	It is after seven
mi esposa amada.	and we are tired of knocking.

The TOWNSPEOPLE *respond:*

Aqui no es meson	This is not an inn,
sigan adelante	keep going down the road.
y no puedo abrir	We cannot let you in;
no sea algun tunante.	you may be a fraud.

At this JOSEPH *and* MARY *turn away and the* CHILDREN *sing:*

Ya se va Maria	So away Mary goes,
muy desconsolada	sad and abandoned
porque en esta casa	because in this house
no le dan posada.	no lodging is given.

On the journey to the second house, another Christmas song is sung by all. At the second house JOSEPH *knocks and sings:*

No seas inhumano.	Open, don't be so cruel!
Tenos caridad	Show us some goodness.
que el Dios de los cielos	Our God has a rule
to lo premiara.	to pay every kindness.

The TOWNSPEOPLE *respond:*

Ya se pueden ir	Go away rare stranger;
y no molestar,	don't insist to knock.
porque si me enfado	Should we lose our temper,
os voy a apalear.	we'll hit you with a rock.

At this JOSEPH *and* MARY *turn away and the* CHILDREN *sing again:*

Ya se va Maria muy	So away Mary goes,
desconsolada	sad and abandoned
porque en esta casa	because in this house
no le dan posada.	no lodging is given.

On the journey to the third house, another Christmas song is sung by all. At the third house JOSEPH *knocks and sings:*

Venimos rendidos	I'm a tired traveler
desde Nazaret.	coming from Nazareth,
Yo soy carpintero	Joseph, a simple carpenter
de nombre Jose.	seeking a place to rest.

The TOWNSPEOPLE *respond:*

No me importa el nombre	Of no importance is your name.
dejenme dormir	Nazareth we do not know.
pues que ya les digo	To us, all are the same,
que no hemos de abrir.	and our only answer is no.

At this JOSEPH *and* MARY *turn away and the* CHILDREN *sing again:*

Ya se va Maria muy	So away Mary goes,
desconsolada	sad and abandoned
porque en esta casa	because in this house
no le dan posada.	no lodging is given.

Singing another carol, the sojourners make their way to the fourth house. Once there, JOSEPH *knocks and sings:*

Posada te pide	Not for myself do I fear,
amado casero	but for this heavenly Queen.
por solo una noche	Her hour is very near.
la Reina del Cielo.	Please hurry and let us in.

The TOWNSPEOPLE *respond:*

¿Pues si es una Reina	If she is a Queen with might,
quien lo solicita?	who made the royal invitation?
¿Como es que de noche	And why so alone at night
anda tan solita?	in such a delicate situation?

Again, JOSEPH *and* MARY *turn away. The* CHILDREN *sing the refrain:*

Ya se va Maria muy desconsolada porque en esta casa no le dan posada.	So away Mary goes, sad and abandoned because in this house no lodging is given.

Another carol or verse is sung on the way to the fifth house. There, JOSEPH *knocks and sings:*

Mi esposa es Maria es Reina del Cielo, y madre va a ser del Divino Verbo.	Mary, the Queen, is my wife, seeking refuge this night. She comes to give life through her son, our light.

The TOWNSPEOPLE *respond:*

¿Eres tu Jose? ¿Tu esposa es Maria? Entren peregrinos no los conocia.	Welcome, Joseph and Holy Mary! We did not recognize either. Pardon for not giving glory or thanks to the fairest Mother.

JOSEPH *replies:*

Dios pague, senores, vuestra caridad, y asi os colme el cielo de felicidad.	May God crown you and bless your kindness. May He love you and fill you with gladness.

The TOWNSPEOPLE *answer:*

¡Dichoso la casa que abriga este dia a la Virgen pura la hermosa Maria!	Happy is the house that is blessed this night by the Holy Spouse and the brightest Light.

The procession enters into the house (the church if the procession took place outside; the manger setting if the procession was inside). The lights are dimmed and all sing:

Entren Santos Peregrinos. Reciben este rincon. Que aunque es pobre la morada os la doy de corazon.	Come in Pilgrims holy; enter and take your rest. Though our home is lowly, we are glad to be blessed.

Cantemos con alegria	Let us sing this story,
todos al considerar	as we are rejoicing.
que Jesus, Jose, y Maria	Jesus, Mary and Joseph
nos vinieron hoy a honrar.	have brought us their blessing.

Members of the procession position themselves appropriately at the manger scene, all the lights are turned on, and a final prayer is said. If this is done for a liturgy on Christmas eve, then the children can take their places up front in reserved seats so that the liturgy itself can begin.

Adaptation

As mentioned before, many variations of this celebration are available. We highly recommend the book *Posadas: The Journey from Nazareth to Bethlehem* by Sister Celestine Castro.

Community Celebration

If Los Posadas is not celebrated as part of the Christmas Eve liturgy or if it is celebrated after the liturgy, an excellent conclusion to the evening is a gala feast with a piñata and pastries and hot chocolate. In keeping with the Christmas theme, the piñata can be in the shape of a star, ornament, or Christmas tree. Although piñatas abound in the Southwest, they may be less available in other parts of the country. We recommend checking import stores far enough in advance to have one ordered if nobody is able to create or find one.

Epilogue: A Little Parable
(revised, with a lovely little change)

Once upon a time, there was a kingdom, right here on earth. In this kingdom lived many people, both big and little. Once a week, all the people were invited to come to a celebration. All the people (well, almost all) would gather together for the celebration. You see, at the celebration, there were many gifts to be unwrapped and some of the big people would unwrap a few of their gifts. The little people of the kingdom had grown a little reluctant about attending the celebration. There were never any gifts for them to unwrap and they felt left out. The big people were beside themselves as to what they could do. They all met to discuss the problem. No one could come up with a solution. Then suddenly, through the doors of the meeting hall, a lone little person entered. The little person came up and stood in front of all the big people and announced in a loud voice, "The problem with all of you big people is that you lost too much of your little." The little person then walked out and the hall was filled with silence. So the big people thought and thought and then they all came up with a great idea.

It was time again for all the people to go to the celebration. Everyone was invited to come, especially the little people. They were told there would be many gifts for even the little people to unwrap. The little people couldn't wait to get to the celebration. Upon arriving, the little people were asked to open any gift they wanted to. Some of the little people opened the gift of hospitality because they loved to smile and welcome all the people as they arrived. Some of the big people even enjoyed the laughter and happiness they were greeted with when they entered the gathering place. Other little people unwrapped the gift of singing, and their gift of song filled the gathering place with beautiful music. Some of the little people unwrapped their gift of serving and carried up the candles and prepared the table for the meal. A few little people unwrapped the gift of gift-bearing and carried the gifts of bread and wine up to the leader during the celebration. There were gifts of eloquent voices unwrapped by some of the little people and then shared by all the people during the storytelling time. When the time came for the leader to talk, gifts of drama, mime and puppetry were unwrapped and shared. The big people couldn't believe all the many gifts that were unwrapped that day.

When the celebration was over, there was a new and exciting atmosphere both inside that gathering place and outside where all the big people met to share. This time, though, all the people, both big and little, were sharing the Good News—for of such is the kingdom.

The Beginning

Appendixes

Children's Liturgies

Liturgy and Children

Every parish eventually encounters the "problem" of children's behavior during Sunday liturgies. Many parishes seek to resolve this "problem" by providing a nursery during the Mass time. However, if the "problem" can be viewed from another perspective, it will become an "opportunity" not only for the children but also for the adults.

The church has made it quite clear that children's preparation for and participation in liturgy is important. The liturgy document *Directory for Masses with Children* is well worth the time it takes to read in its entirety; however, for your convenience the following are a few pertinent passages.

From the Introduction

The Church must show special concern for baptized children who have yet to be fully initiated through the sacraments of confirmation and eucharist as well as for children who have only recently been admitted to holy communion....In the upbringing of children in the Church a special difficulty arises from the fact that *liturgical celebrations, especially the eucharist, cannot fully exercise their inherent pedagogical force upon children....*Nonetheless, we may fear spiritual harm if over the years children repeatedly experience in the Church things that are barely comprehensible... [emphasis added].

From Chapter 1:
The Introduction of Children
to the Eucharistic Celebration

A fully Christian life is inconceivable without participation in the liturgical services in which the faithful, gathered into a single assembly, celebrate the paschal mystery....For this reason all who have a part in the formation of children should consult and work together toward one objective: that even if children already have some feeling for God and the things of God, they may also experience in proportion to their age and personal development the human values that are present in the eucharistic celebration. These values include the community activity, exchange of greetings, capacity to listen and to seek and grant pardon, expression of gratitude, experience of symbolic actions, a meal of friendship, and festive celebration....*Various kinds of celebrations may also play a major role in the liturgical formation of children and in their preparation for the Church's liturgical life....*The final purpose of all liturgical and eucharistic formation must be a greater and greater conformity to the Gospel in the daily life of the children [emphasis added].

From Chapter II:
Masses with Adults
in Which Children Also Participate

On such occasions the witness of adult believers can have a great effect upon the children. Adults can in turn benefit spiritually from experiencing the part that the children have within the Christian community. The Christian spirit of the family is greatly fostered when children take part in these Masses together with their parents and other family members....Nevertheless, in Masses of this kind *it is necessary to take great care that the children present do not feel neglected because of their inability to participate or to understand what happens and what is proclaimed in the celebration.* Some account should be taken of their presence: for example, by speaking to them directly in the introductory comments (as at the beginning and the end of Mass) and at some point in the homily. *Sometimes, moreover, if the place itself and the nature of the community permit, it will be appropriate to celebrate the liturgy of the word, including a homily, with the children in a separate, but not too distant, room.* Then, before the eucharistic liturgy begins, the children are led to the place where the adults have meanwhile celebrated their own liturgy of the word. It may also be very helpful to give some tasks to the children. They may, for example, bring forward the gifts or perform one or other of the songs of the Mass....If the number of children is large, it may at times be suitable to plan the Mass so that it corresponds more closely to the needs of the children. In this case the homily should be directed to them but in such a way that adults may also benefit from it [emphasis added].

From Chapter III:
Masses with Children
in Which Only
a Few Adults Participate

...Masses with children in which only a few adults take part are recommended, especially during the week....It is always necessary to keep in mind that these eucharistic celebrations must lead children toward the celebration of Mass with adults....[A]s many children as possible should have special parts in the celebration: for example, preparing the place and the altar, acting as cantor, singing in a choir, playing musical instruments, proclaiming the readings, responding during the homily, reciting the intentions of the general intercessions, bringing the gifts to the altar, and performing similar activities in accord with the usage of various peoples....*In addition to the visual elements that belong to the*

celebration and to the place of celebration, it is appropriate to introduce other elements that will permit children to perceive visually the wonderful works of God in creation and redemption and thus support their prayer. The liturgy should never appear as something dry and merely intellectual [emphasis added].

Liturgy is not designed for children, and a few moments reflection makes it very clear that the core problem for the children is that they are bored. Most of the time, they can't even see what is going on because they are too little to see over the crowd of adults. Perhaps the most tedious part for them is the Liturgy of the Word. So much of what is said goes right over their heads. If the parish facilities permit, taking the children to a special place for their own Liturgy of the Word can be enriching for everyone. You may also want to consider occasional Liturgies with Children. If your parish has never done this before, take the time to do careful planning and make sure the parishioners know well in advance that this will be done. While some adults may balk at the idea, usually once exposed to such liturgies, they find them enriching and realize that their own understanding and participation has been enhanced. Some even look forward to attending these Masses although they have no children participating.

Keep in mind the following when planning to involve children in a liturgy. First, do your homework. Read the *Directory for Masses with Children*. Check out some of the excellent books that have been written about involving children in liturgy. Many interesting and challenging ideas appear in the book *The Liturgy Documents: A Parish Resource* (Liturgy Training Publications). Second, be sure to work closely with your parish priest(s) and the liturgy committee in planning when and how this will be done. The better the lines of communication, the more likely will be the success of your efforts. The support and enthusiasm of other parish leaders will go a long way in helping the larger community to see this as a positive opportunity and help them to realize that their support and encouragement is important.

If you choose to develop a Liturgy of the Word for Children program, try to use the same format that is used for the Liturgy of Word at Mass. In other words, there should be a reading from the Sunday scriptures adapted to the children's level. There are lectionaries for children that will help with this. Have the children learn to sing one of the gospel acclamations commonly used in the parish. Include an opportunity for the children to express their prayer intentions. For a closing prayer to the session, it can be helpful to use one of the prayers the children will hear again during the Liturgy of the Eucharist such as the Lord's Prayer.

Be aware of the time constraints. Whatever you do, it must be completed in time for the children to return to Mass at the beginning of the Liturgy of the Eucharist. Obviously this can be a bit tricky. A simple solution would be to have one of the ushers assigned to alert the leaders working with the children when the adult community begins the general intercessions. This will usually give them enough time to finish the children's session and bring them back to main

church in time for the presentation of the gifts. Having the children leave and return to the main church should be done within the flow of the liturgy. While it may seem expedient to have the children simply assemble in their own worship space before Mass, it disconnects them from the larger community. Consider having the presider invite the children to "go forth" for their own special Liturgy of the Word after the introductory rites. A cross bearer could lead the children out and escort them to their worship space. Especially with very young children, it is important that they be given a choice to go or stay with their parents. After a while, even the most timid will start choosing to go when they hear the other children talking about how much they like it. When the children return to the main church, they will feel more welcome and a part of the larger community if they are allowed to bring up the gifts. The whole group can be part of the procession, and not everyone has to be actually carrying one of the gifts. Again, allow the children an option. Reserve one or two front pews for those who would like to sit up front where they can see better but also let them know that they can return to their parents if they wish.

Appendices A through E provide more information and practical helps for planning children's liturgies in your parish community.

Whatif?

The following poem by Shel Silverstein humorously portrays the anxieties children sometimes have. It sets the stage for a few Whatifs of our own, which can creep into this ministry.

Last night, while I lay thinking here,
Some Whatifs crawled inside my ear
And pranced and partied all night long
And sang their same old Whatif song:

Whatif I am dumb in school?
Whatif they close the swimming pool?
Whatif I get beat up?
Whatif there's poison in my cup?
Whatif I start to cry?
Whatif I get sick and die?
Whatif I flunk the test?
Whatif green hair grows on my chest?
Whatif nobody likes me?
Whatif a bolt of lightning strikes me?
Whatif I don't grow taller?
Whatif my head starts getting smaller?
Whatif the fish won't bite?
Whatif the wind tears up my kite?
Whatif they start a war?

Whatif my parents get divorced?
Whatif the bus is late?
Whatif my teeth don't grow in straight?
Whatif I tear my pants?
Whatif I never learn to dance?

Everything seems swell, and then
The nighttime Whatifs strike again!

The Whatifs can slink into the best-laid plans, swiftly and unexpectedly:
- Whatif the sound system fails?
- Whatif the slide presentation gets knocked to the floor?
- Whatif the Christmas angel forgets her seven-word line—again?
- Whatif the shepherd forgets his costume?
- Whatif the puppeteer is still sick on the performance day?

Sometimes the Whatifs can remind us of something we have forgotten. Take, for example, the story of Angela. One of our best readers, Angela was a poised and graceful child. When it was time for her to begin her reading, she suddenly became worried. It was as though she had forgotten something. Then she turned to the bench she had been sitting on and shoved it over to the lectern and gracefully leaped up onto it to begin her reading. We had forgotten to place the step stool there and she was too short to reach the top of the podium.

Careful preparation, rehearsal, and repeated double-checking will help to limit problems.

However, catastrophes will still occur. No one is totally immune from them and they do help us develop the keen art of improvisation. It's important to remember that a caring faith community can and will overlook the mistakes that are often part of children's presentations. As human beings we are bound to make mistakes simply because we are not perfect. Sometimes it is the mistake that teaches the greater lesson, as the following story illustrates.

At a liturgy in our parish, a family was asked to carry up the gifts during the presentation procession. The deacon and servers had moved to the front of the altar to receive the gifts. The parents handed the bread and wine to the deacon who, in turn, gave the gifts to the servers to place on the altar. Next, the young child should have given the deacon the basket containing the community's financial offering. Instead, she walked around the deacon, climbed the steps to the altar and walked over to the presider seated to the side of the altar. Setting the basket at his feet, she smiled and gave him a huge hug. She turned around and returned to her seat, confident that she has done exactly what the "job description" had asked. Her genuine and sincere love created a touching liturgical moment for the entire assembly.

Children share so much of themselves that it is often difficult to decide exactly who is ministering to whom. May these pages allow you the opportunity to experience the great personal and spiritual enrichment that we have found in this exciting ministry.

Appendix A: Developing Children's Liturgy

As noted in the introduction, those wanting to work with children in liturgy should request, purchase, beg for or borrow—we do not encourage stealing, however!—a copy of the *Directory for Masses with Children* in order to be grounded firmly in the church's perspective in this important area. The next thing to invest in is a *Lectionary for Masses with Children,* which was approved by the National Conference of Catholic Bishops in 1991. This is one of the most important resources you need for children's liturgies. As in a regular lectionary, the readings are arranged for the liturgical cycles, but they are designed to provide better understanding and comprehension for young people. In addition, it includes readings for special feastdays, weekday celebrations, and sacramental celebrations. A twenty-seven-page introduction provides instructions for young readers about their ministry.

These scripture readings in a simpler language introduce children to the stories told down through the centuries of our faith history. Once young people become familiar with these stories, they are able to associate them with their own life experiences and feelings. Because children typically think concretely, it is paramount to good liturgy that they be able to capture the message in some simple concept or symbol. As they grow older, they begin to use abstract ways of thinking to remember the message and deepen their understanding of the scriptures. This maturing is one of the main goals of children's liturgies. As the *Good News* can only be lived when it is understood, different approaches to assist young people in understanding are needed. Parents involved in their faith communities acknowledge that one hour a week at religion class is simply not enough for a child's faith development. In addition to living their faith at home, children must be able to live it in the regular worship of the faith community. Allowing them to take greater part in the community worship is more than a nice idea; it is an important aspect of their ongoing faith development and sense of belonging to the faith community.

A Child's Faith Development

Psychologists tell us that children have different growth levels, with corresponding differences in faith development. Preschoolers, ages three to five, are at an age of fantasy. They imagine; they draw. They play "grown-up" and strive to imitate whatever adults do. In their faith, they are very much into love—love of God, self and family. They experience their faith through emotions and feelings. Their short attention span and their need for reassurances about their own self-worth are key factors in creating liturgy that speaks to them. Drama or puppet programs can be one of the best methods of capturing their attention. It is even better when they can enter into the story through participating in song, dance or hand gestures.

Development of personal values and conscience mark the growth pattern of the lower elementary grades (first through third). At this age, children are just beginning to become aware socially. They begin to form friendships; they are spontaneous and usually full of energy. It is during this time that a sense of their own self-esteem should be emerging. But it is also at this time that their fledgling self-esteem can be shattered irreparably. A sense of faith is beginning to form in them, as is an awareness of the world around them. These are the most enthusiastic candidates for liturgical ministry. They can do almost all ministries: choir, lector, server, greeter, gift bearer. They can also participate effectively in drama, mime or puppetry. Allowing them to take an active part in liturgy nourishes their sense of self-worth by allowing them to belong.

At the upper elementary grade levels (fourth through sixth), children are beginning to work comfortably in groups and have a need to be accepted by everyone. They enjoy being recognized and mastering new responsibilities. Their faith development becomes more down-to-earth, realistic and practical. They begin to search for more authentic answers for their own beliefs. These children are discovering more of their talents, gifts and abilities. They ask more questions about their faith and are not content with pat answers that don't make sense. They are willing and excited about participating in liturgy, where they can claim ownership, find recognition and feel accepted by in their faith community.

Making Faith a Lived Experience

Most children in a church community have heard the Good News and can tell you the stories of scripture quite well. Does this knowledge, however, give life to their faith? Has this Good News become old news that took place centuries ago, with little or no meaning and value for today's child? We need to retell salvation history to children (and adults) in a way that allows Jesus to be present in their daily life experiences. The techniques that follow can aid dramatically (no pun intended) in this process.

Through song, a centuries-old ritual joins us to our faith heritage at the same time that it allows us to explore new ways to celebrate the Good News. In liturgy, we come together to communicate with each other and with our God. Ritual, whether it comes from the depth of tradition or rises from the new spirit rekindled in Vatican II, is an integral component of liturgy. It's important, however, to remember that both traditional ritual and modern ritual can be deep expressions of faith.

Simple Enhancements

Music, silence, narration and dance are simple options for the enhancement of liturgy. Children can be taught simple hand gestures, or they can clap their hands to the beat of the music. They can sing rounds that are quick to learn and often packed with simple but powerful faith messages.

Storytelling

As children, we would sit on the front porch of a house owned by a little old lady named Mrs. Johnson. She held us spellbound for hours, telling us story after story. She captured our attention and introduced us to using our creative freedom to imagine.

Something very magical and mysterious takes place when someone tells a story.

Storytelling has a way of touching everyone; it goes beyond the past and into the future. It integrates history, sociology, anthropology, archaeology and psychology. It is an art that is making a dramatic resurgence today. Like Jesus, who took everyday symbols of life and crafted them into lifestyle-changing moral teachings, today's storyteller must focus on today's symbols to teach. This medium is not so much about teaching facts and knowledge; it is about allowing the listeners to acknowledge the connection between the story and concepts and images in their own lives.

The resources available for good storytelling are as close as the local library. Another excellent resource to tap is the senior population in your community and church. Younger children feel especially comfortable when older adults sit with them and tell stories. Background music or musical instruments can be used to entice the listener's imagination as the story unfolds. Props are also excellent because young children are very visual.

Puppetry

The ability to use puppets to tell a story or teach a lesson has been part of the world's heritage since ancient times. They are still valuable tools for teaching young people today. Children are much more attentive to puppets than they are to humans, especially adults. Thus, the puppets can be excellent devices to use for children's homilies. By giving puppets the honor and dignity of being gospel messengers, we are telling the children that everything has sacred value— even puppets. Puppetry allows us to break open the Good News message in a way that makes it easy for children to identify with the story. The atmosphere of the puppet script is less structured than a formal homily; however, the thinking and internalizing, the laughter and the learning, the excitement and ease with which the message can be presented far outweigh any perceived loss of reverence or respect for the holiness of the worship space. In addition to the objectives already mentioned, a strong puppet ministry also allows young people to participate actively in liturgy by working with the puppets.

Mime and Drama

For centuries before Christ, people mimed as a way of communicating a message or sharing feelings. In those early times, gesture and dance often accompanied the mime. It wasn't until much later that silence became an integral part of miming. Even scripture is replete with examples of mime; the "words" of the message are dramatized rather than spoken. For example, at the Last Supper, Jesus didn't tell the disciples that they should serve one another. He washed their feet. He showed them, in silence, that service was a necessary component of ministry.

Mime commissions those who see it because it calls forth from them an understanding and involvement on an emotional and intellectual level. Coral Nunnery, retreat leader and liturgist, and Sr. Martha Ann Kirk, CCVI, of Incarnate Word College in San Antonio, provided us with our first encounter of this powerful drama form in liturgy. In a unique portrayal of the humanness of Mary, Sr. Martha Ann drew us into the story by capturing our emotions and relating our own feelings to the fear, excitement and surrender with which Mary gave her "yes" to God. With dance and music and mime, she brought us into the story. It was no longer a gospel passage simply read by a lector. Rather, it was faith, and fear, and finally "yes" to all the possibilities, pains and purpose that the birth of Jesus would bring to a struggling world. Each of us present felt the emotions and understood the power of the Word not spoken.

The above methods are all ways in which we can share the Good News with children. At the same time, we must reassure them that they are a vital and important part of the community in which they worship. The children in our faith community must know that their presence is respected by all and that they are valued children of God.

Little Ways to Begin

The first step is to find a couple of people who are interested in involving children in liturgies. Get together with your parish liturgist, director of religious education, and the school principal, if you have one. Share with them your ideas, concerns and hopes. They can help you with resources and practical advice on how to approach this in your parish and the proper lines of communication. The pastor and parish priests should also be involved whenever possible and appropriate. It may be helpful to attend various parish committee meetings both to get their thoughts on your ideas and to gain their support.

Don't be disheartened if there seems to be little enthusiasm at first. Having a Liturgy with Children at a regular Sunday Mass may need to be a future goal. You may want to start by finding simple ways to let the children be more visible and involved at the Sunday Masses. Perhaps the children could be invited to come up after communion for a special blessing. It might be possible to let them be official greeters before Mass or sing with the choir. A Liturgy of the Word for Children program can also help open the door to the idea of the Children's Liturgy. Your parish leaders can help you discover ways to involve the children. It may be wise to have some special weekday Masses before you attempt a regular Sunday Mass. This will give you time to work with the children on learning the various ministries and to discover what works well and what can be improved. It will also let the children become more at ease and confident in their roles.

If your parish has never had a Children's Liturgy, it is important that their first experience be positive. This does not mean that everything must be perfect; in fact, the unexpected little things that happen can be endearing and, at times, bring home a very meaningful message. It does mean that the readers should be able to read clearly and be heard. The song leaders or the choir should be able to stay on key. The children should know what they are doing and when to do it. The community should feel they are participating and not just watching the children put on a show. If people can leave church feeling a little more joyful, a little more enthusiastic, a little more enriched because of this liturgy, then they will be well on their way to accepting the gifts the little ones of the community have to offer.

Joy, enthusiasm and hope are just some of the special gifts children bring to a community when they are allowed to participate and truly be a part of the community. When they are excluded or ignored, both the children and the adults are losers. Adults can lose sight of what it really means to be "become as little children." Children can lose their sense of self-worth and belonging to the community.

A Little Example

In all of this, the unbounded enthusiasm of the children will shine through. There's a saying, "It's the little things that count." Remember, our God doesn't focus on the great big "grand finale" endings but on the little steps along the way. What we have created may not fit all your needs, but we hope there is enough here to enable you to fashion your own program. The format for this liturgy uses the theme "Unwrapping Little Gifts." Even if you prefer to use another theme, the ideas and strategies that follow should help you in the process.

Step 1: A Little Planning. Six to eight weeks before the liturgy, the core team has a planning meeting (see Appendix D for more on liturgy planning). Make this first liturgy a preview of what is to come. Start by selecting a group of children you know are interested in participating. Assign specific roles for the liturgy, such as readers, altar servers, cross bearer, greeters, singers, etc. If there is a choir, have some children join the regular choir practice sessions. Coordinate with your choir director so that some children's music can be used for part of the liturgy. If there is no choir, check with the parish liturgist about how to arrange for appropriate music.

Using the "Unwrapping Little Gifts" theme, plan the bulletin board design. We displayed a giant invitation stating, "You're invited to a little celebration," using bows as the bodies of children and drawing happy faces of boys and girls for the heads. We duplicated the wrapped gift graphic numerous times on the board to illustrate how many little gifts they have to unwrap. Lastly, we wrote "Come and unwrap your gift" along with the date, time, and place.

Write a bulletin announcement, including the following information:

To the children of (*parish name*):

You are invited to a celebration and party next Sunday. Each of us has many little gifts to unwrap. Please come and help us unwrap your gift at the (*date and time*) liturgy.

We will celebrate "Unwrapping Little Gifts" at this liturgy, and the part afterward will be held (*location*).

Parents may attend *only if accompanied by children!*

Insure that someone will deliver the announcement for inclusion in the bulletin. It should appear in the bulletin for the two weeks before the liturgy. If you choose to have a handout for the children, plan when you will prepare and reproduce it. Also decide when the handout will be distributed and assign volunteers to do it. An appropriate handout at this liturgy would be a ribbon given to all children as they enter for liturgy. It can be tied on their wrists or fingers or made into a bow and pinned to their collars. During the homily they will be asked to unwrap their gift. Designate specific tasks to specific people, taking care that all those present have a task to accomplish.

Step 2: A Little Preparing. Two weeks before the liturgy, the core team meets to prepare and photocopy questionnaires (see the end of this section for the reproducible questionnaire) and reproduce sign-up sheets for each ministry. Set up the bulletin board display announcing the liturgy. If there is more than one information center in the parish, have a display for each one. Assign jobs for coordinating a reception after the liturgy where the children and their parents can find out about the ministries open to children. Establish a list of volunteers and call them requesting their help for specific tasks (furnishing refreshments, serving, cleaning up, etc.). Select adult volunteers who are already involved in the various ministries to assist at the ministry displays and to talk to the children about their ministry. There should be areas representing each ministry the children can do (i.e., greeters, servers, gift bearers, cross bearers, altar servers, lectors, puppeteers, dramatists and mimes).

Decorate the tables with pictures and "tools" used in their ministry (e.g., lectionary, procession cross, songbooks, usher badges, etc.). Puppeteers can give demonstrations, and mime and dance ministers, dressed in costume, can show how they perform. Plan to have the children sign up for the training workshops. They might want to sign up for more than one if they choose ministries that don't require a lot of training time, such as gift bearers. Light refreshments and juice can be served; it may encourage people to go to the various tables if each one offers different refreshments. Set a date and time for the "Unwrapping Little Gifts" workshop and be sure that information is given at the reception. Divide up the responsibilities with the core team and make arrangements to touch base with them when they arrive on the day of the liturgy. Practice with the children involved in the liturgy. You may need to schedule an additional practice for those with major roles.

Step 3: A Little Beginning. The day of the liturgy, arrive early, allowing plenty of time to set up for the reception. Make sure that those who will be distributing the questionnaires and handouts have the materials and are in their places. After the gospel, have the homilist invite the children to sit up front so they can see what is happening. A short talk on children's liturgies and the gifts children have to share can be given. The homily could be used to call forth the children to the ministries. Using the theme of "Unwrapping Little Gifts," a good visual would be to have a few children wrapped in tissue paper and a big bow. Inside the wrapping, they will have a sign indicating what gift they can give: song, reading, greeting smile, etc. When they are unwrapped by the homilist, they can tell the community what their gift is and how they will use it to praise God. At an appropriate time during the liturgy, the children and their parents should be invited to the

reception and encouraged to sign up for the ministry training workshops. Allow time to complete the questionnaires so they can be placed in the collection baskets. Make sure the parents and children know the dates and times of the workshops before leaving the reception. Before leaving for the day, schedule a meeting for the ministers and your core team to plan the workshops.

Step 4: A Little Scheduling. Two weeks before the workshops, the core team meets with the ministers to present the format for the workshop. Details for the two-hour workshop training day should be finalized. Write a bulletin announcement to inform children about the "Unwrapping Little Gifts" workshop, making sure to include the following information:

> To the children of (parish name) who are interested in becoming involved in ministry at our children's liturgies:
>
> You and your parents are invited to a training workshop where you can unwrap the gifts God has given you to share with our community.
>
> "Unwrapping Little Gifts"
>
> Date:
>
> Time:
>
> Place:

Plan creative ways to teach and train the children. Prepare commitment papers for the children to sign after attending the workshop. In coordination with the pastor and other appropriate parish leaders, settle on a schedule for children's liturgies throughout the school year. Reproduce copies of the schedule with ministry sign-up spaces for each liturgy. Include the dates and times of practices for the various ministries. Each minister will need copies of the schedule for the workshop. The same ministry displays used at the reception can be used again for the workshops. Also take time at this meeting to evaluate the questionnaires and summarize the results for the public record.

Step 5: A Little Training. The day of the workshops, begin with a prayer, scripture reading or song in the worship center. The ministers can spend a few minutes sharing about their ministry and commitment with the children. They will need to discuss all the responsibilities involved in the ministry. Remembering that children have a short attention span, schedule a break about halfway through the session and have some refreshments. After the break, children who have signed up for more than one ministry can move on the next one. Children who have selected the more involved ministries can return for another hour of practice. Before going home, the children and their parents will need to sign the commitment papers and get a schedule for future practices. They should sign up for a ministry for the year. After the workshop is over, the core team should take time to evaluate the strengths and weaknesses of the day. Make a summary to help with future planning and for the public record. A date and time for the next core team meeting should be scheduled.

Step 6: A Little Follow-Up. One or two weeks later, the core team meets to evaluate the entire process for creating interest in children's liturgies. After reviewing the sign-up sheets, set up the schedule for the coming year and make copies to mail to the children. Begin planning for the next liturgy. In light of the scripture readings for that liturgy, select a theme. Call and remind the ministers to notify the children involved in the next liturgy. It may be helpful to set a monthly date for both planning and practice meetings for the year.

Checklist: Little Steps Along the Way

		Step 6: A Little Follow-Up (1-2 two weeks after workshop)	☐ Meet with team for workshop and liturgy evaluation. ☐ Review sign-up sheets. ☐ Copy and mail sign-up sheets to children. ☐ Plan next litrgy (date, time). ☐ Study scriptures. ☐ Ministers call children in next liturgy. ☐ Set monthly date to plan future liturgies.	
		Step 5: A Little Training (day of workshop)	☐ Arrive early to set up. ☐ Invite children and parents to sign commitment papers. ☐ Sign up children for liturgies for the year. ☐ Send home schedules of practice. ☐ Schedule next team meeting.	
		Step 4: A Little Scheduling (2 weeks before workshop)	☐ Convene meeting of liturgy team and members. ☐ Plan training workshop. ☐ Schedule liturgies for year. ☐ Evaluate questionnaires. ☐ Send place, time, and date of workshop to office for inclusion in bulletin.	☐ Copy commitment papers. ☐ Copy sign-up sheets for liturgy. ☐ Copy practice schedules. ☐ Plan refreshments for workshop.
	Step 3: A Little Beginning (day of liturgy)	☐ Arrive early to set up. ☐ Assist at liturgy. ☐ Set date for meeting. ☐ Assist at reception.	☐ Encourage all to sign up. ☐ Give dates of workshop. ☐ Collect questionnaires. ☐ Invite ministers to meeting.	
	Step 2: A Little Preparing (2 weeks before liturgy)	☐ Convene a team meeting. ☐ Copy questionnaires and sign-up sheets. ☐ Prepare bulletin board. ☐ Set date for one more practice. ☐ Make necessary handout decisions and divide up liturgy responsibilities.	☐ Call volunteers to serve at reception. ☐ Select adult ministry leaders (ushers) for reception. ☐ Practice liturgy.	
Step 1: A Little Planning (6-8 weeks before liturgy)	☐ Hold first meeting and select children. ☐ Plan bulletin board. ☐ Plan liturgy and handout for next liturgy. ☐ Set date for next meeting. ☐ Write up announcement for bulletin and turn in to office.			

Children's Liturgy Questionnaire

Please fill out and place in the collection basket.

1. Are you and your family interested in having a children's liturgy on a regular basis? If so, how often would you like to see children's liturgies celebrated in our parish?

    ☐ weekly   ☐ bi-monthly

    ☐ semi-monthly   ☐ quarterly

    ☐ monthly   ☐ other

2. Has the message of the Good News been helpful for you and your family at the children's liturgies we have celebrated so far?

3. Are the children's liturgies meeting your needs and the needs of your family?

4. Would you and your family be interested in participating in the children's liturgies?

5. Do you have any ideas or suggestions that would help the liturgy to be more beneficial to the children?

Appendix B: Little Ministry Tasks

What follow are descriptions of the responsibilities that can be part of the ministries available to children. As in everything, your parish may do things differently.

The key to success in this important and valuable ministry of children's liturgies is flexibility. Adapt this list to the individual style of your faith community.

Greeters

This is a ministry of hospitality. In some parishes, it is combined with the role of usher; in others, it is a separate ministry. The major responsibility of the greeter is to welcome people as they gather for worship. Having special nametags identifying the children as greeters helps to reinforce that they are ministers to all who are present. It is often significant to have an entire family involved in this ministry. Following are some responsibilities that can be included:

- greeting people as they enter church
- helping people find places to sit
- directing people to the nursery and restrooms
- distributing hymnals and worship aids and collecting them after Mass
- handing out the bulletins
- passing the collection baskets
- guiding people to communion

Cross Bearers

This ministry involves participation in the gathering rites, entry and recessional processions. The best age for this ministry is fourth grade and up. Responsibilities include carrying the cross at the beginning and end of the liturgy.

Gift Bearers

Those involved in this ministry carry up the gifts of the assembly. At least three children should be used for this ministry. More children can be involved when there are special gifts in addition to the bread, wine and collection. This can also be a family ministry.

Altar Servers

The servers assist the presider throughout the liturgy and are responsible for special tasks before and after Mass, such as lighting and putting out the altar candles. The training needed is more involved and there may already be a program in place in your parish. It is important to establish good communication lines with the coordinator of altar servers, if this is the case.

Lectors

Lectors are responsible for presenting the scripture readings and general intercessions during the Liturgy of the Word. The readings and intercessions may be presented by one lector or they may be divided among two or three lectors. Lectors will need to commit to at least one practice during the week before the liturgy. This practice should include instructions on their place in the entrance and recessional processions and where they are to sit. It is wise to have the children come early on the day of the liturgy for a final reading practice. To help insure that nothing goes wrong, you may want to have an adult sit up front to assist them.

Art and Environment Ministers

Adults and children of all ages can participate in this ministry. The main objective is to enhance the atmosphere for each liturgy. Responsibilities include the following:

- preparing banners and handouts
- decorating bulletin boards
- readying the lighting, sound system and props
- making sure things are set up before the Mass and taken down after

Dancers

Dancers and other children can be used to carry streamers or banners, which help bring color and movement to the liturgical procession.

Dramatists or Mimes

In this ministry, the Good News is proclaimed by acting out a skit, presenting a mime, dancing or storytelling. This ministry may also include adult homilists. Participants will need to commit to a few rehearsals before the day of the liturgy. They will also need to arrive early to set up and to stay after to clean up.

Puppeteers

This ministry provides a message about the Good News. Usually two practices are necessary before the liturgy. Responsibilities include arriving early for a final practice and setting up and dismantling the stage. The recommended age for this ministry is ten-fifteen years old.

Choir Members

An essential part of the liturgy, this ministry involves the congregation in worship. The foremost responsibility is to attend scheduled practices and arrive at the liturgy early for warmups. Children should be able to read before volunteering for this ministry. Dorothy Ybarra, choir director at St. Brigid's Parish in San Antonio, offers these notes:

- The key is careful organization, advanced planning and lots of help! The most important point to emphasize is to make the experience enjoyable. Maintain a positive approach and recognize what is done well. Mistakes should not be ignored but should be worked with in a non-punitive way, preserving the dignity of all involved.

- A long-range approach assists you in the day-to-day planning and allows you to give the attention needed to specific seasonal music. Children usually catch on to a new song quickly, but it's highly likely they will not remember it by the next rehearsal. Allow plenty of time for repetition of the piece prior to the "big day."

- Preparation is critical for teaching children a new piece of music. Plan how you will divide the song into teachable phrases. Introduce the entire song by either singing it yourself or playing a tape. Then, teach the song by singing each phrase and having the children echo it. Be sure to "string" the phrases they are learning to the ones they have just learned, eventually putting together the entire song. After the initial learning process, go through the entire song a couple of times with accompaniment. Correctly introducing a new song will save time in the long run. Correct mistakes early and don't be afraid to teach dynamics and phrasing right away.

- Good music in liturgy is essential, because badly performed music is distracting for those to whom you are ministering and embarrassing to the choir performing it. Learning the music and performing it correctly is only part of making this ministry a meaningful, enriching experience for the children. It may be helpful to teach the children about the meaning of the various parts of the liturgy and why some parts are sung rather than spoken, as well as the meanings of various words or phrases in the songs. Take the opportunity to teach them both the meaning and pronunciation of new words. Make sure that the children enunciate clearly. In fact, work on exaggerating correct pronunciations when they sing because sound dissipates as soon as it is created. No matter how well the notes and rhythm are performed or the words are expressed, all is lost if the children cannot be heard. Work carefully with creating balance between the instruments and the children's voices. Microphones to amplify voices, multi-level risers, and an acoustic shell are all possible ways to enhance children's liturgical music by strengthening the quality of the children's voices.

Appendix C:
Let the Little Children Come (A Survey)

In order to better meet the needs of the children, we visited religion classes at a few church communities, asking children some questions about children's liturgy. We weren't surprised by their answers, as young people are wise and their suggestions creative. We'll share their answers here to highlight some of the problems and solutions children's liturgists face.*

The important thing to gather from this is the variety and diversity of the children's responses, not to mention their sense of humor. This survey should also strengthen you in your efforts to bring children's liturgies to life. You can conduct a similar survey in your own faith community, using the reproducible handout at the end of this section.

Why do you come to church on Sunday?

- To learn about God.
- To celebrate with God and friends.
- To respect God.
- To listen to the readings.
- My parents made me.
- To honor God.
- Jesus wants us to be there.
- To make friends.
- To ask God for another chance.
- To sing songs to God.
- To pray for the poor.
- To say good morning to God.
- To see friends.

What do you like most about liturgy?

- Singing.
- Praying.
- Listening to the readings.
- Shaking hands and sharing peace.
- The whole children's mass.
- When the priest comes down to talk to us.
- Sitting by friends.
- Being a cantor in the choir.
- When mass is different.
- When we eat the bread and drink the wine.
- The end of liturgy!
- When the deacon shakes your hand.
- When she sleeps.
- Spanish songs.
- When a baby is baptized.
- When the three kings came.
- When we let the balloons go up at Easter.

How do you feel about children being a part of liturgy (choir, greeter, server, puppets or drama)?

- It's fun.
- It helps you understand it more.
- It seems shorter when you help.
- You get to meet a lot of people when you are a greeter.
- I'm happy when I read the stories, so it isn't so boring.

---

* The children who participated were of all nationalities; approximately 60 percent of these children were Hispanic. The questionnaire was presented at several parishes in the same geographic area.

- We feel special when we get to help.
- I don't have to sit with my parents.
- They give us a chance to learn.
- We sing songs I really know.
- You can feel how the older people feel.
- You feel good about it.
- I actually get to do something.
- I like to answer the questions when the priest asks them.
- Moving around is better.
- It's an easier way to learn about God.
- It's more exciting.
- I liked it when I was an angel at Christmas liturgy.

What do you think we could do to make liturgy better?

- Sing more songs.
- Make it not so long.
- Ask the kids more questions.
- Make it bigger so more people could come.
- Give more money to the church for the poor.
- Go to liturgy with a smile on your face.
- Make a bigger nursery for the babies.
- Get something special.
- Have an ice cream stand.
- Not to say the same thing over and over again.

- Just not let the children in.
- Have a fifteen minute break.
- Be able to talk to friends.
- Have other people talk for homily.
- Not have liturgy go into overtime.
- Have more children a part of it.
- Stop all the sitting and standing—either sit or stand.
- Let the kids dance.
- Put in a jungle gym.
- Make the readings easier to understand.
- The celebrant should tell a story.
- Use more kid words.
- Make it one hour shorter.
- Have Father not talk so long.
- No singing.
- Have more children's liturgies.
- Skip homily.
- Puppet shows.
- Kids do mass for a day.
- Get more seats so no one will have to stand.
- Have toys to play with.
- Make mass a party.
- Have refreshments after mass.
- Barbecue after liturgy every three months.
- Go on field trips.

Parish Survey

(No names, please.)

What do you like most about liturgy?

How do you feel about children being a part of liturgy?

What do you think we could do to make liturgy better?

How old are you? (Optional)

☐ 5-7
☐ 8-10
☐ 11-14
☐ 15-19
☐ 20-29
☐ 30-50
☐ over 50

Parish Survey

(No names, please.)

What do you like most about liturgy?

How do you feel about children being a part of liturgy?

What do you think we could do to make liturgy better?

How old are you? (Optional)

☐ 5-7
☐ 8-10
☐ 11-14
☐ 15-19
☐ 20-29
☐ 30-50
☐ over 50

Appendix D:
Planning the Children's Liturgy

It will be helpful to develop a consistent format for your liturgies. Give a copy of the Children's Liturgy Planner to all who are involved, including the presider, liturgist, liturgy coordinator, director of religious education, choir director, and any other volunteers. Liturgy goes well when everyone involved knows the plan.

Children's Liturgy Planner

Preliminaries

Date, Time, Theme. These three items allow you to categorize, organize and file this planner for future information and planning.

Date _____

Time _____

Theme _____

Scripture Readings.

First Reading _____

Second Reading _____

Gospel Reading _____

Details

Lighting, Audio-Visuals, Sound System. These three elements create the atmosphere for the drama or mime. It is important to have a person assigned to dim the lights at the appropriate time. Similarly, assign someone to run the following, if used: slide projector, cassette recorder or sound system, overhead projector or special spotlight. It is essential to test all equipment *before* the liturgy as well as to walk through each step with the volunteers.

Lighting _____

Audio-visual equipment _____

Sound system _____

Altar. Keep in mind that the altar or holy table, where the eucharistic celebration takes place, must always be inviting those gathered to come to the paschal banquet. If it is covered with banners, flowers and decorations, it does not welcome the assembly; rather, it gets lost behind the decorations.

Altar _____

Other Environment. The props or puppet stage need to be in place before liturgy begins and easily moved away after the homily without a lot of distraction. Display larger visual aids outside the church or in the gathering space, if your church has a large one. Those gathering for worship will see the displays as they come to liturgy and again as they leave.

For example, for a Thanksgiving liturgy or food drive, a table covered with a cloth could be displayed in front of the church. On the table a bushel basket turned on its side, with a harvest of fruits and vegetables and large loaves of bread cascading from it, could visually remind the assembly of the need to be generous. Or a bright red wagon (ideal for a children's liturgy) could be set out with canned goods placed in it. As the people gather for liturgy, they can add their gifts. The wagon can then be pulled up to the altar at the presentation of the gifts.

Smaller displays such as handouts or duplicated copies of the symbol for the theme of the liturgy can be placed throughout the worship space. Using the same Thanksgiving theme, the worship space could be decorated with small clusters of fall leaves or wild berries in vases near the altar, taped to the ends of the pews, on or around light fixtures, etc. The obvious caution here is that too much of a good thing isn't good!

Banners that grow or change each week, used during the seasons of Advent or Lent, need to be displayed where everyone can see them. These are excellent transformation symbols that capture the children's attention each week as they come to liturgy. The best place for the banners would be off to one side of the altar or by the ambo.

Other (banners, etc.) _____

_____

Hospitality

Greeters. This ministry is so vital to the community. Greeters need to arrive about thirty minutes before liturgy. Their job is to greet individually all those gathering for worship and give them a hymnal, songbook or bulletin (if it is your church's custom to distribute the bulletin before the liturgy). The greeters will need their best smiles and the ability to extend warm welcomes to all. You may want to schedule a few extra helpers when you are giving out handouts before the liturgy.

Greeter(s) _____

Handouts (optional)_____

Ministries

Servers. Scheduled in advance and properly trained, young servers do a great job in this ministry. It is important to communicate well with the director or coordinator of servers so that duplications and overlaps don't occur. Respecting the needs and timelines of other ministry coordinators is essential to the success of children's liturgies.

Servers _____

Cross Bearer. Select a young person who is strong enough to carry the processional cross (if one is used) and set it by the altar. This may take some practice and is less easy than it appears.

Cross Bearer _____

Introductory Rites

Greeting. This is a brief welcome to the assembly. It calls all to worship. The child who welcomes needs to have an exuberant voice that lets all gathered know it is time to begin.

Greeting _____

Entrance Song. This song is led by the children's choir. It is important, however, to encourage the assembly to participate. The song gathers the community and sets the mood for listening to the Good News of the day. The song needs to create a sense of celebration and is the vehicle through which the assembly hears the theme for the liturgy.

Entrance Song _____

Penitential Rite. This rite can be sung by the choir or read by the presider. It may need to be written so that the children can comprehend the words and their message.

Penitential Rite _____

Gloria. This song may be sung by the choir, but it can also be recited. One possibility is to sing the Gloria on special feasts or seasons (Christmas, Easter) and recite it on other occasions.

Gloria _____

Opening Prayer. The celebrant takes this time to pray for all gathered a prayer that again speaks to the theme of the liturgy.

Opening Prayer _____

Liturgy of the Word

First Reading. The child selected to read the story of God's people should wait until all have settled and are quiet. It is essential that the child has practiced beforehand and is comfortable in a speaking role. The concept is that the reader give reverence and dignity to the Word.

First Reading _____

Responsorial Psalm. It is preferred that this be sung—if not the entire psalm, at least the refrain. Variations include using a psalm tone chant or playing lightly on instruments while the reader reads the verses.

Responsorial Psalm_____

Second Reading. This reading, always from the New Testament, is also read by one who has prepared and practiced beforehand. This reading, too, must be proclaimed with great dignity.

Second Reading _____

Gospel Acclamation. This acclamation is generally sung by the choir, then repeated by the assembly. It should proclaim to all: "Stand up and hear the Good News." Its mood should be upbeat, festive and joyful. However, if it is not sung, it should be omitted entirely.

Gospel Acclamation _____

Gospel. Usually, this passage is proclaimed by the presider or deacon. It can be mimed or dramatized with a narrator at the ambo and the actors visible to all. If done in drama, the presider may use a simple gesture to have the assembly sit down.

Gospel _____

Homily. The children are invited to come forward and gather in front of the worship space. If your church does not have the luxury of space near the front, you will need to improvise. Perhaps the children could stand or move forward up the aisles. Allow enough time for everyone to find a space before beginning the homily. After the homily is over, greeters can distribute handouts to the children as they return to their families. This is also the time for volunteers to move forward so that props and the puppet stage can be quickly removed, as well as any other equipment. If this is done smoothly and quickly, it will not distract from the liturgy. A helpful hint is to attach the script of the drama or puppet show to the liturgy planner so that, should something go wrong, it will be handy.

Homily _____

General Intercessions. One way for the children to take ownership of their liturgy is to encourage them to write their own petitions, with leadership and guidance from their teachers. Your faith community may have a coordinator for this ministry, so again remember that good lines of communication are essential to the success of this particular prayer. A deacon or lector or a few of the children can read these intercessions, and the response can be read or sung. Traditionally, these intercessions focus our prayers on four areas: the church, nations and leaders, all people in special need, and our own community's needs.

Liturgy of the Eucharist

Preparation of the Gifts. The greeters pass the baskets for the collection.

Preparation of the Gifts _____

Gift Bearers. Select in advance a few children or a family to carry up the gifts to the altar.

Gift Bearers _____

Presentation Song. Led by the children's choir, this hymn need not mention the bread and wine or offering. It may also be called the Song for the Preparation of the Gifts. It can be one of praising and rejoicing. If a song is used during the homily, an instrumental version of the same song may be played as the gifts are being gathered and the table is prepared.

Presentation Song_____

Eucharistic Prayer. Eucharistic prayers written especially for use at children's liturgy are available and are more appropriate for children's liturgies. In addition, many versions of these prayers are set to music with repetitive responses that the children can quickly learn. Excellent versions by Carey Landry may be found in *Young People's Glory and Praise* (North American Liturgy Resources).

Eucharistic Prayer _____

Holy, Holy, Holy. The children's choir leads the community in this hymn of praise.

Holy, Holy, Holy_____

Memorial Acclamation. The choir and the assembly join in this hymn of praise.

Memorial Acclamation _____

Great Amen. This is usually sung by all; the children's choir may use a simple version that children can easily sing.

Great Amen_____

Lord's Prayer. A practice particularly successful at children's liturgies is for the entire assembly to pray this prayer together as children of the Lord united together as one.

Lord's Prayer_____

Sign of Peace. All exchange a handshake or a hug.

Sign of Peace_____

Lamb of God. This prayer may be spoken or sung by the children's choir and the assembly. Some maintain that singing here stacks up too many songs with virtually no space in between; others maintain that this piece needs to be sung because it is part of the service music—specific, unchanging prayers used at every liturgy. New music for this prayer incorporates a litany of eucharistic titles in a repetitive setting.

Lamb of God _____

Communion Song. This song should be simple and unifying. It is a time of celebrating the realization that each of us is a member of the Body of Christ.

Communion Song_____

Communion Meditation. This time can be set aside for a period of silence or a meditative song.

Communion Meditation _____

Prayer after Communion. The presider prays this prayer, which usually links the eucharistic celebration with the day-to-day lives of those gathered for worship.

Prayer after Communion _____

Concluding Rite

Blessing. Before the final blessing, it is beneficial to the children for the presider to repeat the Good News message contained in the theme of the liturgy or puppet skit. This can be one or two sentences reminding them about the main ideas and encouraging them to take the message back to their families, their schools, etc. Then the presider blesses the entire assembly.

Blessing _____

Dismissal. This is done by the priest or deacon. It is in this dismissal, given by the presider or deacon, that we are sent forth in peace and love and challenged to share the Good News with others.

Dismissal_____

Concluding Song. Led by the children's choir, this song is a joyful expression of the entire liturgical celebration. As the children leave, some extra greeters may be needed to distribute the handouts (if this is the most appropriate time for your faith community to do so).

Clean-Up

Clean-Up. Don't wait until the church is empty to start wondering whom you can recruit to help clean up. Plan ahead for what needs to be taken down (banners, puppet stage, slide projector, VCR and TV, props, visual aids, tapes removed from recorder). Encourage your crew of children and adults to get the job done quickly, especially if there is another liturgy beginning shortly.

Clean-up crew _____

Follow-Up

Follow-Up. After the liturgy, try to visit with the parents and children to find out what they liked or disliked about the homily. Jot these notes down, and reflect on your own assessment of the liturgy. These notes will prove helpful when another liturgy is planned. Start a file with your planner. Ideas can be used for homilies, prayer services, retreats or other celebrations.

1. What went wrong?

2. What could have been better organized?

3. What went well?

4. What could have been left out?

5. What could have been added?

Other Notes/Feedback:

Appendix E: A Model Children's Liturgy

Once you have completed all the background work, you are ready to create children's liturgies for your own faith dimension and parish family. The scripts in this book are intended to give you starting places for selected themes, or they can be used exactly as written. As mentioned earlier, although this resource was created from experiences within the Catholic faith, the scripts are inherently about choosing goodness—and every faith seeks that.

The following model, "Unwrapping Little Gifts," is designed to encourage participation in children's liturgies.

Unwrapping Little Gifts

Theme

- To call forth children to share their gifts in liturgy.

Scripture

- Ephesians 4:7-12
- 1 Timothy 4:14

Setting

- liturgy or other worship service

Props

- tissue paper
- ribbon to wrap up the children
- questionnaires for parents to complete

Characters

- homilist (priest, religious education director or guest homilist)
- 2 or 3 children wrapped as a present with bows

Suggested Music

- "Jesu, Jesu, Fill Us with Your Love"
- "Bloom Where You're Planted"
- "Children of the Lord"
- "We Are Many Parts"
- "Love That Is Kept Inside"

Suggested Handout

- Ribbon: As the children enter for liturgy, tie a ribbon around their finger or wrist, or distribute a bow that can be pinned on the collar (if manufactured bows are used, the backing can be peeled off and the bow stuck to the collar).

Presentation/Homily

The homilist can begin by reading one of the suggested scriptures. The main idea of this presentation is to call forth the children to unwrap their special gifts. The homilist should share with them that they all have gifts inside of them. The homilist can call the children who are wrapped up as presents to come forward and be unwrapped, saying, "Let's unwrap (*name of child*) and see what gift he or she has to share." The first child can be unwrapped and say, "I have the gift of song. I love to sing and I want to share my gift in the choir." That child can sing a short tune. The homilist unwraps the next child and asks him or her to share a specific gift; it could be a good voice to read, and the child could read a line of scripture. The next child could be unwrapped to share his or her big smile, a sign of the gift of hospitality for greeting before liturgy.

After all the children have been unwrapped and have returned to their seats, ask all the children to close their eyes and think for a few minutes about what gifts they may have to share in liturgy. It would be helpful to name the ministries. As the children do this, ask the parents to take a few minutes to answer the questionnaire, which they will later place in the collection basket. The choir can sing a selection from the suggested music or play background music.

Invite the children and parents to a reception following the liturgy.

Resources

Books and Periodicals

Better Homes and Gardens Mexican Cook Book. Des Moines: Meredith Books, 1977.

Buscaglia, Leo. *Living, Loving and Learning.* New York: Fawcett, 1985. See especially the quotation by Frederick Moffett, Bureau of Instructional Supervision, New York Department of Education, "How a Child Learns," page 154.

Castro, Celestine. *Posadas: The Journey from Nazareth to Bethlehem.* Available from the Mexican American Cultural Center Bookstore, P. O. Box 281185, 3000 W. French Place, San Antonio, TX 78228. Telephone (210) 732-2156.

———. *The Story of Our Lady of Guadalupe.* Available from the Mexican American Cultural Center Bookstore, P. O. Box 281185, 3000 W. French Place, San Antonio, TX 78228. Telephone (210) 732-2156.

Jamison, Andrew. *Liturgies for Children.* Cincinnati: St. Anthony Messenger Press, 1975.

Groome, Thomas. *Christian Religious Education: Sharing Our Story and Vision.* New York: Harper and Row, 1980.

Johnson, Thomas H., ed. *The Complete Poems of Emily Dickinson.* Boston: Little, Brown and Company, 1890-1960.

Kelemen, Julie. *Advent Is for Children: Stories, Activities, Prayers.* Liguori, Missouri: Liguori Publications, 1988.

Kirk, Martha Ann. "Liturgical Drama." *The Dictionary of Sacramental Worship.* Edited by Peter E. Fink. Collegeville, Minnesota: The Liturgical Press, 1990.

The Liturgy Documents: A Parish Resource. 3rd ed. Chicago: Liturgy Training Publications, 1991.

Malloy, Patrick. "Whose Liturgy Is It?" *Today's Liturgy* 14: 5-6.

Munsch, Robert. *Love You Forever.* Ontario, Canada: Firefly Books, Ltd., 1986.

National Conference of Catholic Bishops. *Committee on the Liturgy* 27 (November/December 1991).

Silverstein, Shel. "Whatif." *A Light in the Attic.* New York: HarperCollins Children's Books, 1981.

Weems, Ann. "Silver Spoons." *Reaching for Rainbows.* Philadelphia: The Westminster Press, 1980.

Music

The music resources here are listed alphabetically by song title, with publication information following.

"Abba! Father!" by Carey Landry. North American Liturgy Resources, 1977.

"Amazing Grace" by John Newton, arranged by Henry Papale. North American Liturgy Resources, 1985.

"Are Not Our Hearts" by Carey Landry. *Glory and Praise Hymnal.* North American Liturgy Resources, 1973.

"Be Thankful." *Psalty's Non-Stop Singalong Songs* cassette. Maranatha! Music, 1988.

"Beginning Today" by Darryl Ducote, Damean Music, 1973. Published by North American Liturgy Resources.

"Bloom Where You're Planted" by Carey Landry. North American Liturgy Resources, 1979.

"Brand New Song." *God Uses Kids* cassette. Maranatha! Music, 1987.

"Celebrate God" by Carey Landry. *Hi God* cassette. North American Liturgy Resources, 1973.

"Children of the Lord" by Carey Landry. *Young People's Glory and Praise.* North American Liturgy Resources, 1976.

"Children, Run Joyfully" by Bob Dufford, SJ. North American Liturgy Resources, 1977.

"Color the World with Song" by Carey Landry. North American Liturgy Resources, 1982.

"Come Along with Me to Jesus" by Carey Landry. North American Liturgy Resources, 1983.

"Come, Lord Jesus" by Carey Landry. North American Liturgy Resources, 1976.

"Come O Lord." *This Is Our Faith Hymnal.* Silver Burdett & Ginn, 1988.

"Come to My Heart" by Joe Pinson. North American Liturgy Resources, 1981.

"Dona Nobis Pacem" by Mary Miche. *Peace It Together: Peace Songs for Kids* Song Trek, 1980.

"Fingerprints" by Mary Rice Hopkins. *Fingerprints* cassette. Krystal Records, 1988.

"Follow Me." *Jesus Put a Song in My Heart* cassette. Silver Bells Music, 1986.

"Gettin' Ready for the Miracle" by Linda Rebuck and Tom Fettke. *Gettin' Ready For The Miracle.* Lillenas Publishing Co., 1986.

"Gifts in My Heart." *This Is Our Faith* Hymnal. Silver Burdett & Ginn, 1985.

"God Is a Surprise" by Harry H. Pritchett, Jr. Oakhill Music Publishing Co., 1974.

"God Uses Kids" by Peter and Hanneke Jacobs. *Colby #4/God Uses Kids* cassette. Maranatha! Music, 1987.

"Grandma's House" by Mary Rice Hopkins. *Fingerprints* cassette. Krystal Records, 1988.

"Heart to Change the World." *Psalty's Non-Stop Singalong Songs* cassette. Maranatha! Music, 1988.

"He's Still Working on Me, You've Got to Try." *Jesus Put a Song in My Heart* cassette. Silver Bells Music, 1986.

"His Banner over Us Is Love" by Carey Landry. North American Liturgy Resources, 1973.

"I Am Only One." *This Is Our Faith Hymnal.* Silver Burdett & Ginn, 1988.

"I Like Me" by Carmino Ravoa. *This Is Our Faith Hymnal.* Silver Burdett & Ginn, 1985.

"Jesu, Jesu Fill Us with Your Love." *This Is Our Faith Hymnal.* Silver Burdett and Ginn, 1990.

"Jesu, Jesu Fill Us with Your Love" by Tom Colvin. *This Is Our Faith Hymnal.* Silver Burdett & Ginn, 1969.

"Jesus Christ Is Risen Today." *This Is Our Faith* Hymnal. Silver Burdett and Ginn, 1990.

"Jesus Is with Us Today" by Owen Alstott. *This Is Our Faith Hymnal.* Silver Burdett & Ginn, 1989.

"Jesus, Jesus" by Carey Landry. North American Liturgy Resources, 1976. Recommend especially verses 3, 4, and 5.

"Joy Is My Strength—Give It Away" by Mary Rice Hopkins. *Fingerprints* cassette. Krystal Records, 1988.

"Joy, Joy, Joy." *Psalty's Non-Stop Singalong Songs* cassette. Maranatha! Music, 1988.

"Kids Under Construction." *Jesus Put a Song in My Heart* cassette. Silver Bells Music, 1986.

"Let Heaven Rejoice" by Bob Dufford, SJ. North American Liturgy Resources, 1972.

"Let There Be Peace on Earth" by Sy Miller and Jill Jackson. Jan-Lee Music, 1955.

"Lord Is My Shepherd, The." *This Is Our Faith Hymnal.* Silver Burdett & Ginn, 1979.

"Love." *Music Machine* cassette. Sparrow Records, 1989.

"Love That Is Kept Inside" by Carey Landry. North American Liturgy Resources, 1973.

"May We Grow." *This Is Our Faith Hymnal.* Silver Burdett & Ginn, 1981.

"My Shepherd Is the Lord" by Jack Miffleton. North American Liturgy Resources, 1983.

"Oh, Yes, Lord Jesus Lives" by Carey Landry. North American Liturgy Resources, 1976.

"Our God Is a God of Love" by Carey Landry. North American Liturgy Resources, 1981.

"Peace." *Music Machine* cassette, Sparrow Records, 1977.

"Peace Is Flowing Like a River" by Carey Landry. *Comprehensive Glory and Praise Hymnal.* North American Liturgy Resources, 1975.

"Peace of the Lord, The" by Gary Ault. *Young People's Glory and Praise.* Damean Music, 1976. Published exclusively by North American Liturgy Resources.

"Peace Prayer" by John Foley, SJ. *Glory and Praise Hymnal.* North American Liturgy Resources, 1984.

"Peace Prayer" by John B. Foley, SJ. *Comprehensive Glory and Praise Hymnal.* North American Liturgy Resources, 1976.

"Peace Time" by Carey Landry. North American Liturgy Resources, 1973.

"Psalm of the Good Shepherd (Psalm 23)" by Carey Landry. North American Liturgy Resources, 1982.

"Reach Out" by Carey Landry. North American Liturgy Resources, 1973.

"Service" by Buddy Ceasar. Damean Music, 1969. Published exclusively by North American Liturgy Resources.

"Sharing Comes Round Again" by Mary Rice Hopkins. *Fingerprints* cassette. Krystal Records, 1988.

"Signs of New Life" by Carey Landry. North American Liturgy Resources, 1979.

"Sing a Simple Song" by Peter and Hanneke Jacobs. Maranatha! Music, 1976.

"Sing a Simple Song (Joey's Song)" by Carey Landry. North American Liturgy Resources, 1976.

"Smile." *Music Machine* cassette. Sparrow Records, 1977.

"Smile!" by Les Waguespack and Carey Landry. Maranatha! Music, 1979.

"Thank You, God." *Hi God!* cassette. North American Liturgy Resources, 1973.

"Thank You, God, for Being So Good" by Carey Landry. North American Liturgy Resources, 1982.

"This Little Light of Mine." *Psalty's Non-Stop Singalong Songs* cassette. Maranatha! Music, 1988.

"Violet in the Snow" by Don Mayhew. North American Liturgy Resources, 1975.

"Walk with Jesus" by Mary Rice Hopkins. *Fingerprints* cassette. Krystal Records, 1988.

"We Are Many Parts" by Marty Haugen. *Gather Hymnal.* GIA Publications, Inc., 1980.

"We Come to Share." *This Is Our Faith Hymnal.* Silver Burdett & Ginn, 1988.

"Wedding Banquet, The." The Medical Missionary Sisters, 1965.

"Welcome to the Family." *Psalty's Non-Stop Singalong* Songs cassette. Maranatha! Music, 1988.

"What We Need in This World Is." *This Is Our Faith Hymnal.* Silver Burdett & Ginn, 1988.

"World Is a Rainbow, The" by Mary Miche. *Peace It Together: Peace Songs for Kids* Song Trek, 1980.

Spanish Music

Cantos para Pedir Posadas y Otras Canciones de Navidad by Sister Celestine Castro. Copyright 1982. Available from the Mexican American Cultural Center Bookstore, P. O. Box 28185, 3000 W. French Place, San Antonio, TX 78228. Telephone (210) 732-2156.

Danos Senor de Esos Panes by Carlos Rosas. Available from the Mexican American Cultural Center Bookstore, P. O. Box 28185, 3000 W. French Place, San Antonio, TX 78228. Telephone (210) 732-2156.

Rosa Del Tepeyac: Misa en honor de Nuestra Senora de Guadalupe by Carlos Rosas. Copyright 1976. Available from the Mexican American Cultural Center Bookstore, P. O. Box 28185, 3000 W. French Place, San Antonio, TX 78228. Telephone (210) 732-2156.

Una Espiga: Canticos de gracias y alabanza by Cesareo Gabarain. Oregon Catholic Press, 1984.

Index of Scripture References

Unwrapping Other Gifts

Developed by the Benedictine Resource Center

MINISTRY TO HOMEBOUND:
A Training Course

Kent C. Miller

Paper, 8½" x 11", 144 pages, $29.95
ISBN 0-89390-329-9, June 1995

Everything you need for a ten-session course on ministering to the homebound: background on building a caring ministry, session plans, and reproducible handouts. Sessions include: Making a Visit, How to Be Caring, Communicating Care, Practicing the Presence of God, Active Listening, Prayer As Part of Ministry, Prayer for Wholeness and Healing, Understanding Grief, Special Challenges in Visitation, and Ministry to Dying Persons.

LAYING THE FOUNDATIONS
OF MINISTRY

Kent C. Miller

Paper, 8½" x 11", 125 pages, $29.95
Spiral bound, ISBN 0-89390-333-7

Everything you need to organize and implement ministry in health and wholeness. From secretaries to stockholders, all members of the community can help to bring about healing, and *Laying the Foundations* can help you employ these valuable resources.

DEVELOPING A HEALTHY LIFESTYLE

Janice L. Burggrabe & Kent C. Miller

Paper, 8½" x 11", 254 pages, $34.95
Spiral bound, ISBN 0-89390-334-5

Developing a Healthy Lifestyle is designed to support and encourage individuals within congregations to unwrap their gifts for ministry to teach and lead others in making healthy lifestyle choices. This manual offers ways the congregation can learn about their individual health and lifestyle choices. Its focus is on being balanced, being centered, and being connected as ways to live a healthy Christian life. The leaders are given content and methods, with ample handouts for members of a class or group. Can be used for retreats, regular meetings, or church adult education classes.

INVOLVEMENT IN PUBLIC POLICY

Nancy Amidei

Paper, 8½" x 11", 135 pages, $29.95
Spiral bound with tabs, ISBN 0-89390-335-3

To improve your parish health, you might need to change public policy, and you can if you know what you're doing. *Involvement in Public Policy* tells you how. With it, you'll learn how bad public-policy decisions are hurting your parish community. You'll find out how public policy is made at local, state, and federal levels. And you'll get some tools that will help individuals and committees organize to have an impact. With the health-care system in flux, this is a resource you don't want to be without.

Order from your local bookseller, or use the order form on the last page.

GOD MADE ALL OF ME:
Activities for Young Children

Jolynn Johanning

Paper, 8½" x 11", 90 pages $11.95, Illustrated, ISBN 0-89390-210-1

Cassette $9.98, Separate Songbook $9.95

More than 30 activities for preschool and primary school children. Use as a supplement to your regular catechetical text or as a help if you're creating your own program. Chapters on creation, bible stories, family, Advent, Christmas, Lent, Easter, forgiveness, and Eucharist. Includes permission to photocopy activity sheets. The accompanying music collection, written especially for 4-7 year olds, includes a Mass setting and 27 songs that complement and can be used with the activities. Arrangements by Steven Farney.

BREAKING OPEN THE WORD—CREATIVELY!
A Video Resource for Catechists

Monica Brown

Edition for Catechists Working with Elementary-Aged Children:
118 minutes, VHS, $49.95

Edition for Catechists Working with Youth:
110 minutes, VHS, $49.95

The vignettes on these videos give you plenty of ideas about how to make your teaching more exciting and more effective. Includes an introduction on incorporating creativity into your teaching.

I'M GOD'S CHILD: 27 Songs for Young Children

Lesley Clare

Paper, 8½" x 5½", 64 pages, $7.95, ISBN 0-89390-196-2
Two accompanying cassettes $19.95
Book and cassette set $26.95

These songs and activities will help young children (ages 3-7) grow in faith. Many of the tunes are familiar with updated lyrics, made inclusive and simplified for children. Includes actions and activities that get children involved in the music.

THE LORD BLESSES ME

Dick Hilliard

Paper, 8½" x 11", 152 pages, $12.95, ISBN 0-89390-005-2

Based on the lectionary, *The Lord Blesses Me* contains more than 200 ideas and activities for celebrations with young children. Includes 40 complete celebrations for the seasons of Advent and Christmas, Lent and Holy Week, covering all three cycles (ABC).

Order from your local bookseller, or use the order form on the last page.

CELEBRATING THE LECTIONARY (CTL), a unique curriculum designed especially for Roman Catholic parishes, helps you accomplish your catechetical mission in three important ways:

1 First, CTL makes it easy for you to coordinate catechesis for all age levels. It has five catechetical packets for children/youth and one for adults (especially useful for small faith communities, general Bible studies, and catechumenate).

2 Second, CTL is economical. Simply order one teaching packet for each class. Catechists use the lesson plans and photocopy as many activity sheets as needed. (The sheets are included in the packet.) No need to guess how many students you'll have in September. No need to bust the budget on textbooks and workbooks. And best of all, the packets cover the whole year so you don't have to reorder every few months.

> *"Scriptures are coming alive for our children and our teachers. Lessons are effective and deal with 'life-death' issues of the children. Attendance is consistently high and growing."* — Shirley Birchak, Sacred Heart, Spokane, Washington

3 Third, CTL maintains a clear distinction between catechesis and liturgy. Although there is an interplay between catechesis and liturgy, their primary purposes are different. The purpose of catechesis is to teach. Thus, the editors have provided lesson plans designed to help you provide an educational experience for children and adults. The purpose of liturgy is to gather as a people and worship God. Therefore, the editors have provided an outline for Children's Liturgy of the Word designed to allow children to celebrate God's word at their own level. The editors hope you will use both programs—the catechetical and the liturgical—and have designed them to complement each other. Children's Liturgy of the Word is not a substitute for catechesis—any more than going to "religious-education class" is a substitute for going to church.

...in Six Great Catechetical Packets

The six catechetical packets are the heart of Celebrating the Lectionary. Each packet contains everything the catechist needs (with the exception of some music resources) to lead a lectionary-based session for each Sunday of the school or calendar year.

The five catechetical packets for children and youth cover each Sunday from September through June of the next year.

The Adult Catechetical Packet covers each Sunday from September through August of the next year. This flexible packet can be used for catechumenate, general Bible study, Re-membering Church, lector preparation, and small faith communities.

All catechetical packets carry the Imprimatur of the Diocese of San Jose.

NURSERY
Ages 3 to 4
$59.00

BEGINNER
Ages 4 to 6
$59.00

PRIMARY
Ages 7 to 8
$59.00

INTERMEDIATE
Ages 9 to 11
$59.00

JUNIOR/SENIOR
Ages 11 to 15
$59.00

ADULT
Ages 15 and up
$69.00

CHILDREN'S LITURGY OF THE WORD
Ages 6 to 9
$69.00

FAMILY HANDOUT MASTERS
English or Spanish
$30.00

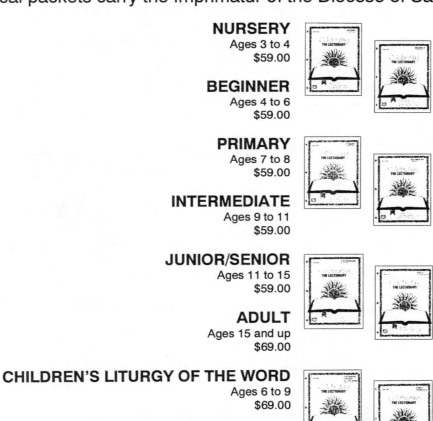

Stories in the Language of Children

BALLOONS! CANDY! TOYS! and Other Parables for Storytellers

Daryl Olszewski

Paper, 5½" x 8½", 100 pages, $8.95, ISBN 0-89390-069-9

Olszewski tells nine delightful stories, then shows readers how to tell these stories in preaching and teaching, how to come up with new stories, and how to make stories into faith experiences for children.

PARABLES FOR LITTLE PEOPLE

Paper, 5½" x 8½", 100 pages, $7.95, ISBN 0-89390-034-6

MORE PARABLES FOR LITTLE PEOPLE

Paper, 5½" x 8½", 82 pages, $8.95, ISBN 0-89390-095-8

both by Lawrence Castagnola, SJ

With imaginative parables, Castagnola's positive message helps reach children in preaching, in teaching, and in the simple pleasures of storytelling. Sixteen parables in the first volume; fifteen more in the second.

TELLING STORIES LIKE JESUS DID: Creative Parables for Teachers

Christelle L. Estrada

Paper, 5½" x 8½", 104 pages, $8.95, ISBN 0-89390-097-4

Bring home the heart of Jesus' message by personalizing the parables of Luke. Each chapter includes introductory comments and questions, an easy-to-use storyline, and discussion questions for primary, intermediate, or junior high grades.

Song and Prayer

CELEBRATING OUR JOURNEY

Monica Brown

Cassette $9.98, Songbook $9.95

This collection, featuring "The Emmaus Song" and "From a Long Way Home," captures the essence of Scripture, spirituality and experiences for children. Includes songs suitable for catechesis, gathering, or closing—as well as a full Mass setting for children.

SUNDAY'S CHILDREN: Prayers in the Language of Children

James Bitney & Suzanne Schaffhausen

Cloth, 6" x 9", 72 pages, $9.95, ISBN 0-89390-076-1

These children's prayers are ideal both in the classroom and in the home. The authors wrote these prayers to give children a feel for talking to God naturally, which encourages their own spontaneous prayer. A great resource for teachers, librarians, and parents.

- -

Order Form

Order these resources from your local bookstore, or mail this form to:

QTY	TITLE	PRICE	TOTAL
	_____		
	_____		
	_____		
	_____		
	_____		

Subtotal: _____

CA residents add 7¼% sales tax (Santa Clara Co. residents, 8¼%): _____

Postage and handling
($2 for order up to $20; 10% of order over $20
but less than $150; $15 for order of $150 or more): _____

Total: _____

Resource Publications, Inc.
160 E. Virginia Street #290 - LF
San Jose, CA 95112-5876
(408) 286-8505
(408) 287-8748 FAX

☐ My check or money order is enclosed.

☐ Charge my ☐ VISA ☐ MC. Expiration Date _____

Card # _____ - _____ - _____ - _____

Signature _____

Name (print) _____

Institution _____

Street _____

City/State/ZIP _____